# ANNA, BLANCHE, THEN ME

*the story of three women, each with their own tale*

*An old family photograph (1916), many individuals unidentified*

*Front Row: Leon, Rheal, Laureda, Blanche (stomach enlarged because of malnutrition), Maurice (note two left shoes), Pomerleau*
*Back Row, Hormidas Pomerleau, three unidentified, Anna Veilleux (hiding from camera because she was pregnant with Helena).*

Photo on cover and title page is a family photo owned by the author.

Cover design by Mary Helen Miskuly.

Book design by Mike Miller, pubyourbook@gmail.com.

ISBN: 9781692365486

For my grandchildren:

Christopher Allen, Monica LeCou Bacon,
Marianna Allen, Matthew Allen,
Christy Rose Pieroni, Nicholas Pieroni,
Anna Victoria Nicolia,
Frank Miskuly, Mary Katherine Miskuly.

And for my great-grandchildren:

Shelby Allen, Charlotte Allen, Louis Bacon,

If you don't know where you come from,
You don't know where you're going.

~Sadie Roberts-Joseph

# CONTENTS

# ANNA

I am but a grain of sand in the universe,
moved by the tides of life,
soon to disappear.

My grandmother, Marie Anna Veilleux, was one of eleven children, a common happening in Catholic Quebec. Her father Joseph, a prosperous merchant, did not approve of the handsome blonde scalawag who came to court and win his sheltered and religious daughter. Her new life would be very different from the comfortable surroundings of St. Georges de Beauce. Her home had been in a bustling community, with sisters and brothers, aunts and uncles, and many cousins to gossip and share secrets. The big white wooden house sat high up on a hill, facing the road and the swift flowing Chaudiere River. With so many children, the house was always a beehive of activity, and sometimes Anna found it pleasant to just be alone. Her favorite time and place to dream was in the spring, sitting in the white lacy gazebo in the side yard of the big house. The tendrils of the wild sweet peas would be just beginning their annual climb up the sides of the white lattice and, by late summer, they were so thick that they choked off most of the sunlight in the interior space. The parish church was just a short walk away. From a very early age she began her routine of going down one hill and up the next, to say her prayers at morning mass. Daily, her brother-in-law Armand Morin provided a heavenly ambiance, playing the big pipe organ brilliantly, in spite of the fact that he was missing a right thumb.

My grandfather Hormidas wooed and won my grandmother Anna, and in June of 1903 he brought his petite nineteen-year-old bride to the outskirts of a small village twenty miles from her parent's home. Anna's new home in Quatre-Chemins was a small, rundown shack with a dirt-floor, tucked away from any neighbors. Her first baby, unnamed, was born and died before her first year marriage anniversary. Her next child was a sickly boy named Ferdinand born in 1906. Leon was born in 1907. When Leo was one year old his two-year old brother Ferdinand died. Three months later in 1908, my mother, Blanche, was born. Rheal was born in 1910, followed by Maurice in 1912, then Laureda in 1913. Helena was born in 1916.

Anna's day always began before dawn. She would dress, comb and tie up her long thick black hair, and then go to the kitchen to revive lasts night's fire in the wood stove. She would go outdoors to relieve herself in the outhouse, then go to the outdoor pump to wash her face and hands and get water for the porridge and tea. This ritual continued in every season because that stove was used for both heating and cooking. Next, she would start making the bread, so it could rise before kneading and baking. When the children got a little older, she would go to the back shed, scattering the clucking chickens on her way, and harness their only horse to the caleche or buggy, a wedding present from her father. With a light flick of the whip, the horse was alerted to begin the trip to the parish church of St. Prosper three miles away.

My mother recalled that every day of the winter before her mother died, even in the fiercest of blizzards, she would never miss that long ride to church. Her life was hard, but she believed it was God's will. Hormidas would sleep through it all, still feeling the effects of the moonshine that he and his backwoods friends enjoyed the night before.

Anna's husband was not ambitious. He sold small bundles of wood to people in nearby St. Prosper, made moonshine deep in the forest and, in the spring, along with other family members and a few neighbors, made maple syrup. I treasure a family picture taken when my mother was just eight. I have often wondered who had a camera and who took that picture which captured it all. The setting was the Quebec woods in late spring. Blanche, her blonde hair a mass of frizz, stands in front of a wooden lean-to, with her brothers and sisters. My grandfather has a clay pipe in his mouth and stands in the second row with some other unidentified people. The heavy woman on the end of the row leans both elbows on a large upside-down snowshoe. In the picture, the only part of my grandmother that is visible is her head peeking behind the third row. She was carrying her sixth child and thought the camera would injure the child's soul. In the picture my mother clutches her brother Maurice by one hand, with her sister Laureda on the other side. Maurice wears two left shoes. Blanche's belly is bulged out because of malnutrition. A young man licks a wooden spoon dripping with syrup. There are seventeen people in the picture, and each pair of eyes look blank, each visage sad, weary and without hope. In the early spring of 1916, each of these faces showed the toll of a hard winter and the daily survival around a wood stove, eating bread with the staple molasses, an egg when the chicken was laying, and little else. That was poverty.

Anna died at the age of thirty-four because of exhaustion and consumption. Her small frame was laid out in the kitchen on two wooden planks held up by two dirty sawhorses. Her unkempt chestnut hair cascaded over the wooden edge. Dried, brownish red blood had crusted in the corner of her tiny mouth. It was June in the backwoods of Quebec. Black flies buzzed my grandmother's corpse as my mother Blanche led her three brothers and two sisters into the dirt-floored kitchen to kiss their mother in a final goodbye. There was no money to bury my grandmother in the local parish of St. Prosper, so with a heavy heart, her father came from St. George de Beauce to bring his daughter's hand-made oak casket back to St. George to be blessed and buried in his family plot behind the church on the second hill.

# BLANCHE

My mother had to become the heart and soul of the family. There was to be no more childhood for my mother. At twelve years old she made the meals, baked the bread, tended the garden and picked the wild berries. She made the lye soap with which she washed the clothes by hand. She kept the stove burning, but most of all, she embraced her five brothers and sisters, especially Helena, the beautiful bright-eyed baby of the family.

Helena was only four when her mother died. One day Hormidas announced that he had decided that there was one too many mouths to feed, and so he made arrangements to take her to a cousin in Lawrence, Massachusetts. He would take her in a wagon filled with hay and smuggle her across the United States border. It would be thirty-four years later that she and my mother would be reunited once again.

Throughout her life my mother had vivid nightmares which always ended in her terrible moans and screams. As she got older family members would harness her in a flat position, because she would throw herself violently from her bed. I asked her many times what was the subject of her recurring dream, but she would never say. When she was in her 80's she finally revealed her lifelong vision of her father chasing her in the woods, lifting up her skirt with a stick, a signal that he was going to violate her.

Not one of the remaining five children had the opportunity to go to school. My mother went to second grade. When she was eighteen my grandfather Hormidas announced that he was about to take a new wife. He made the decision to have my mother go and live with her aunt Clara Morin in St. George de Beauce. The boys Leon, Maurice, and Rheal and the remaining daughter Laureda would remain with the new wife. My mother stayed with her aunt Clara for the next two years. When she was twenty, she followed the Chaudiere River north, walking the sixty miles along the river's edge to Quebec City. She had heard from her cousins that the Chateau Frontenac Hotel was hiring French Canadian girls as chambermaids. The penniless blonde beauty was immediately hired.

When the Chateau Frontenac Hotel was built by the Canadian Pacific Railroad in 1893, it became the symbol of English superiority over the French. Perched high on the cliff of Quebec overlooking the St. Lawrence River, it imposed an impressive silhouette to the poor French who lived in small stone houses on one of the narrow winding streets of the lower town.

In 1928 the French were the illiterate workers, most of whom were imported from the surrounding farms and countryside. The French religious, both priests and nuns, conducted themselves a step above the French inhabitants. In fact, the Ursuline Convent was in the upper town, only a few blocks from the Chateau. They had control and policed the thinking and mores of the French residents. The American writer Henry Miller visited Quebec City with his wife June Mansfield in 1928, just a few months before he visited Europe for the first time. In a May postcard he wrote "everywhere we went we seemed to bump into flocks of nuns or priests. Lugubrious-looking creatures with ice in their veins."

The English, who made up forty percent of the population at that time, were members of the government and were the professionals of the community. There was a definite class distinction which many years later, has resulted in great animosity among the educated French Canadians of modern times. In 1928 many of the wealthy English were permanent residents of the chateau.

My mother Blanche entered into this new world with hope and enthusiasm. Many of her cousins had also come to work at the hotel, and they provided a busy network to receive the news and gossip of the family and friends left behind in the province of Beauce. She wanted to elevate her life. She was a keen observer. Always handy with a needle, she took mental note of the latest fashions worn by the English residents, then recreated "the look" with a purchase from a local thrift shop, a practice that would continue throughout her life. She was happy for the first time. Heads always turned when she walked by. One of those heads was that of the son of a local physician who lived at the chateau. My mother never revealed his name to me. He was studying to follow in his father's medical footstep when he met and fell madly in love with the beautiful Blanche. What's more, he wanted to marry her. The father told his son that it was quite impossible to accept a French-Canadian chambermaid into their elegant circle of family and friends. They continued to tryst for almost a year in spite of his family's objections, meeting in the shadows of a darkened church or in the crowd of one of the many festivals and concerts centered around the chateau. Suddenly her happiness was shattered. She received a message from her brother Maurice that their sibling Leon, one year older than herself, had contracted tuberculosis and needed immediate medical care. At aged twenty-one he was dying. He would need to be transported from his home in St. Prosper to Sherbrooke, Quebec, where the Sanatorium would provide an environment of medical attention, rest and proper diet. To her, this was a financial crisis of the greatest proportions.

My mother met this challenge by meeting with her suitor's father and cutting a deal. She was a realist. She knew that her marriage into this family would never really happen. She would just speed up the parting to her own advantage. She promised never to see his son again if the doctor would make the arrangements and financially provide for the care of her brother. He readily agreed and carried out his end of the bargain. She met with her broken-hearted lover for one last time. He gave her a delicate crystal ring topped by a single ruby when they parted, and it is now a cherished part of my patrimony.

***

Six months later, a message was left with the hotel operator saying that her brother Leon was dead. The cousins she worked with pooled their money, so she could travel to make his burial arrangements and buy a casket. She first went to Sherbrooke by train to retrieve his body and then took the body to the Cathedrale Marie-Reine-du-Monde in Montreal for a Mass and burial. Blanche told the priest that she had no money left and could not pay for the Mass. The Cure's response was that her brother's casket must remain in the back of the church during a regularly scheduled Mass. This incident was the first piece of kindling that would smolder and then, given fuel many more times, would finally ignite into her lifelong lack of respect for the Catholic Church.

***

When she returned to Quebec City there was another message waiting for her. Her sister Laureda, now eighteen years old, was in trouble and needed help. In the rural villages of Quebec, the parish priest served as a kind of mayor and moralist. Local populations believed that his word was the word of God. He was the law. It seems that the parish priest of St. Prosper had decided that her sister was a "bad girl". He decreed that she should be taken to the Ursuline Convent in Quebec City to be rehabilitated. My grandfather and his new wife were in complete agreement. Besides, it was one less mouth to feed. My mother was shocked to find out that her sister was being held as a prisoner in a convent basement located just a few short blocks from the chateau where my mother worked. She was being forced to do laundry for the English gentry for her room and board. This was deemed to be penance for her evil ways. At the first opportunity, my mother rushed over to the convent and demanded to see her sister. Laureda was allowed to speak to my mother through a wrought iron grille. She sobbed and begged my mother to get her out. My mother tried, but to no avail. A few months later, another message was left for my mother. It was from the convent. My Aunt Laureda had intentionally allowed herself to fall down a steep flight of basement stairs. The nuns wanted no more part of her and told my mother to come and get her sister.

When I inquired as to the veracity of this story, Marie-Andree Fortier, Archiviste of the Monastere des Ursulines de Quebec wrote to me:

> I am the archivist of the Monastery des Ursulines de Quebec. Following your call yesterday, I made a research in the newspapers of the community, and in a list of the employees of the monastery for 1927 to 1932. I looked for a mention of Loretta's names either Laureda or Loreda Pomerleau, and I found nothing. If she worked in the laundry of the monastery to pay for some sins, there is no written mention of this. On the other hand, it does not mean that it is false. It is possible that the situation was not written by the nuns simply because they did not consider this a major fact in the history of the community.

My mother returned to the hotel, sister in tow. There was always menial work at the Chateau but the paltry pay included room and board. Laureda hated her job. She had to work so hard and was paid so little. Three months later she left in the middle of the night, hopping a train to Montreal. My mother followed, dragging her back to Quebec City. By this time, her sister had tasted the interesting fast life and quick money of the "red light" district of St. Catherine Street. It was only a short time before she ran away again. Montreal was to be her lifelong home. My mother could do no more.

Aunt Laureda said she was a waitress, but I'm not convinced. She met her husband who was then serving in the Canadian Merchant Marines. She became pregnant, and to his credit, he married her. He became the youngest captain in the Merchant Marines of Canada, and then became Harbour Master for the port of Halifax. Although he never lived with my aunt, he was generous in his support of my aunt and their son.

Meanwhile, in Quatre-Chemins her brother Maurice had grown to be a strapping, six-foot young man. At nineteen, he had dreams of a better life away from his dreary village. He decided to follow the river north to find my mother and all of the possibilities that the busy city might bring. When he arrived at the chateau, he had no place to stay. My mother shared a room with her cousin Lillian, and they agreed to hide Maurice in their room each night. He would disappear during the day, look for work and then return to his sister's room at supper time. After their days work the cousins would each slip into the hotel kitchen, taking leftover food from the plates of the guests and residents, and return to their room where Maurice would devour the stolen feast.

Each day Maurice left to try to find a job. Chances of employment were very slim because one third of all of Canada's population was unemployed. One damp and gray autumn day, he saw a crowd of people gathered on one of the street corners. It was a bread line, so he stepped into the serpentine row that stretched down the cobbled block. With nothing else to do, he inched his way towards the front of the line. Volunteers with bowls and ladles were serving soup with a slice of bread. One volunteer distinguished himself from the rest. Dressed in fine grey tweeds and a warm wool scarf, he seemed to be in charge. He stared at my tall handsome uncle as he approached the steaming pot of soup. The gentleman beckoned to Maurice to come over to see him.

"What is your name, lad?" the man said in French with a thick Scottish brogue.

"Maurice Pomerleau, sir," my uncle replied.

"Have you ever attended school?" questioned the older man.

"No sir," was the reply. My uncle Maurice hung his head.

"My name is Gordon MacNab, and I could use another worker, but first you must make me a wee promise. You must agree that you will go to school and that I will hold back some of your wages as savings for your future. I have room at my house. Are we agreed?"

My uncle could not believe his good fortune. He agreed to meet Mr. MacNab at 4 p.m. He ran back to the chateau to try to find my mother and tell her his good news. He wrapped his few belongings into a sweater, swung the small pack over his shoulder, and dreamed about his future. From that day forward, his life would be forever changed. Mr. MacNab had no children and when he retired several years later, my uncle who used to wear 2 left shoes, was able to buy the company, the largest asphalt company in the Province of Quebec.

# THE ROYAL YORK HOTEL, TORONTO

In 1933, a group of fifteen French Canadian chambermaids, under the watchful eye of their motherly French-speaking chaperone Madame Alice LaFleur, boarded a CPR train in Quebec City to begin a new life adventure at this much talked about city and new hotel. My mother and three of her cousins were in that group of excited French girls. The train stopped in Montreal to board more passengers. The girls stopped their giggling long enough to observe a dapper new fellow, my father, who looked like the current movie heartthrob, Clark Gable, right down to the Brylcreemed jet black hairline with the perfect “widow’s peak”, to the hazel brown eyes and perfectly groomed mustache. I’m sure that his clothes were old and used, but he would wear them with much aplomb. He always did.

He entered their train car carrying a very strange package. It was a large turkey wrapped in brown butcher paper, the headless long plucked neck dangling down from the edge of the paper. The most recent new passenger immediately noticed the beautiful blonde. He sat himself down in the caned wooden seat behind my mother, the wrapped turkey firmly placed in his lap. The train pulled away from the Montreal station and the girls began to chatter again.

I have no idea why or to whom that bird was going to in Toronto, but I do know that Jack Huard, my father, was going to look for a job as a butcher in that expanding city. But now, on that train, he had to find a way to meet my French speaking mother. He began to move the turkey neck around the edge of the seat in front of him.

"Gobble, gobble," he gobbled out.

Everyone but my mother laughed.

Again, "gobble, gobble".

Still no reaction from my mother. By the time the group got to the Union Station in Toronto, my father had my mother's name and the address of the Royal York Hotel.

In such difficult times, a small cadre of young souls at the hotel became fast friends. Cousin Cecile fell in love with Bill Waters, the tall elegant guy with the curly hair and the watery blue eyes, who worked in the bowels of the building as a Valet. Cousin Lillian met and married Fred Breakwell, the hotel piano man. Her sister Roland met Joe Emman, a recent immigrant from Estonia. My dad was the song and dance man of the group. He had a wonderful voice and knew every word of all of the traditional British vaudeville routines. He was ready to entertain in a heartbeat, always carrying a double harmonica in his left breast-coat pocket. The group got together at every opportunity, Fred playing the piano while my father sang. Jack was always smiling, so upbeat and always the life of the party. His favorite song, which he taught me, and I have always believed, was "The Best

Things In Life Are Free". It was a truism hard to understand during those difficult times.

My father continued to court my mother who never seemed as gay and happy as the rest of the group. He still could not find work, but not because he didn't try. In Toronto in 1934, 30% of the labour force was out of work, and one fifth of the population became dependent on government assistance. At the Yonge Street Mission located at Yonge and Gerrard Streets, men stood five across on the wide sidewalk, in a long line down the street. Every day during the Great Depression, the Mission gave out food and clothing to the thousands who waited for a coat or a beef sandwich with a cup of hot tea. In an old photo of the mission, a large sign hung over the door "FREE BREAKFAST FOR MEN every Sunday morning at 8 a.m.". When did the ladies eat?

The four cousins, already in their mid-twenties, were all in a survival mode, with no thought of having a family. In May of 1935 my mother announced that she and my dad would get married. My mother and father were married at 6 a.m. on the morning of the 22nd of May at a regular morning mass at St. Patrick's Church just a few blocks north of the hotel. The group of six plus my mother and father were all in attendance. Not one of them had any money to pay the priest. No flowers, no party, no honeymoon. Everyone went back to work except for my father Jack.

I was born in October of that year and, in the French tradition, immediately baptized. My father's full name was John Raymond Huard, so I was to be called Raymonde. It was at the baptismal font that my father changed the name to Mary Jacqueline. I never liked my name. My mother's cousin Lillian was my godmother and her cousin Roland's husband Joe was my godfather. The group now had a baby doll to fuss over, but that happiness did not last for very long. My mother was losing weight and was constantly spitting up blood. She was diagnosed with what was then known as consumption and now known as tuberculosis.

What to do? My mother needed medical attention and my father was out of work. The disease was highly contagious and potentially fatal. A nurse from the Provincial Health Department stepped in and put my mother in isolation on a train car located in the Union Station. The station was located directly across the street from the Royal York Hotel. That train took her to the Muskoka Sanatorium in Gravenhurst, Ontario. For the next three years she would receive rest, nourishing meals, and plenty of fresh air thanks to the Canadian government. I think that's where my mother learned to read and write. After all, she had plenty of time on her hands. Jack continued to look for work.

What about little Jacqueline now eighteen months old? To those working in anti-tuberculosis work in the Sanatorium, it was thought that tubercular mothers should be confined, and the offspring could be well looked after apart from her. I would be removed from my mother and father until my mother's health was in such condition that she could look after me without any risk of infection. I was sent to the Preventorium, a 128-bed facility operated by the Victorian Order of Nurses. The hospital was located on the estate of Evangeline Booth, daughter of the founder of the Salvation Army William Booth. Located on Yonge Street north of the city, it was surrounded by fields, woods and farms. This small hospital was organized to care for poorly nourished, underfed children exposed to tuberculosis, and who were living in the midst of the worst conditions that existed in the city. Here children would be given light, air, and proper food.

I entered a truly different world, since all of the staff spoke English and my parents had only spoken to me in French. There are certain things that I remember even though I was very young. I remember the long gray porches located around the second floor of the building where afternoon naps were taken daily, even in the cold of winter. I was a thumb-sucker. Every night I would cry when the nurse put my tiny hand into a tin mitten, which was then attached to the side of the metal crib by two twill cotton ribbons. That should have stopped that dreadful habit. At eight years old I was still sucking my thumb at night and sometimes at hidden moments during the day. Like many experiences in life, there are ways to find comfort. I found love in the form of a nurse called Margaret Johnson. I became her child and she became my mother. Too young to know better, I gave myself to her completely, but she should have anticipated the day when I would leave and be reunited with my family. That happened in 1939, and she was devastated.

That year life for my mother and father would take a positive turn. They rented a small apartment on Winchester Street very close to a Red and White grocery store where my father had finally found a job as a butcher. I was returned to their care. It seemed, to my mother at least, that her life so far had been tough, and she hadn't asked for any of her past trials. There would be no time for tenderness. I can't ever remember a hug or kiss from either my mother or father. My mother spoke to me in French and I answered her in English. She manipulated our small family, and for the next number of years ran our lives as a mini-business enterprise.

I started school at the age of five. My parents found a larger place to rent on Naismith Street, a short street in Toronto's Cabbagetown. In September I began my school years at Saint Martin's, the local Catholic school. I attended for two days. On the morning of the third day, my mother told me that I was going to a different school, one that would require a uniform and a daily streetcar trip. She dressed me and then took me to the streetcar stop, followed by a ride, a transfer, and another streetcar ride. The next day, at five years old, I made the long trip alone to Saint Joseph's College School on the corner of Bay and Wellesley Streets. It would be my school and part time home for the next twelve years.

How did this all happen? St. Joseph's College School was an expensive private school and the provincial motherhouse for the Sisters of St. Joseph in Ontario. My mother never lacked nerve, deceptive charm or imagination. She went to the convent and asked the good sisters to take me in as a "charity" case. They agreed, and they even threw in a used uniform. Now, because I would be gone all day, she could find a job to increase the family income. I would begin a childhood of imposed independence and new adventures on four fronts, my home, the neighbourhood, school and, the very best and the most exciting part, the journey to and from.

# SAINT JOSEPH'S COLLEGE SCHOOL

Saint Joseph's College School was founded by the Sisters of Saint Joseph of Toronto in 1852. The good sisters must have known a bit about real estate because a hundred years later their huge block of downtown property, once known as Clover Hill, would be the nun's ticket to future security. To indicate how big that block was, in 1955 the Provincial government bought the convent and school property for millions and built four very large office towers in that space. The building housed nuns, novices, postulants, and boarding students, most of whom were from South America and northern Ontario. There were also day students who lived in the swanky neighbourhoods north of the school, and then there was me from Cabbagetown.

An eight-foot fence had been built at the edges of the property. The extra wide, horizontal boards were painted battleship gray, broken only by two entry gates around the entire downtown city block. Both gates had an oversized black latch to open the door. When I was younger, I had to stand on my tippy toes and cup both of my small hands together, to push open that latch. It would always close with a very loud decisive clank that seem to say, "you're in for the duration" or "you're out and you can't come back in". The entrance on the Wellesley Street side was used for convent business. The entrance on the opposite side of the block on St. Alban's Street was only opened during school hours.

Being always alone became a new adventure. I always took the streetcar to school in the morning. No excitement there because the streetcars were always jammed with people preoccupied and traveling to downtown jobs. Riders just peered into space, alone with their thoughts and imagination. No cell phones to immerse the traveler. After two streetcars rides, I'd just get off, walk a short block, open that enormous gate latch and then spend time with James the janitor. I was always early, and he was my special friend. He had a very large "T" broom which I would straddle on the brush side, holding on to the handle in the middle, my legs dangling on either side. At five years old I didn't weigh much. He would lift the broom off of the ground, with me on it, and give me a whirl. It was my morning ritual.

From the very first day of school, I was captivated by the spaces between the two latched gates. A cluster of brick buildings, attached by glass alleys, took up most of the yard. One glass hall was named the Madonna Hall, where copies of art pieces painted by famous artists and featuring the Madonna and Child, hung the entire length. Years later I was able to revisit that hall by viewing many of the originals in many of the major museums around the world.

A second glass alley had beautiful patterned terrazzo floors and a series of ten music practice rooms, each with a piano, chair, and metronome. It seemed that there was always someone "making beautiful music". How I yearned to take lessons in one of those tiny rooms, but financially that was out of the question.

The third alley in the school was just before the convent side of the building, a space that, for me, was always full of mystery.

Everyone there was always silent and prayerful, and no one looked you in the eye. Before you arrived at the church-sized chapel, there was a huge wooden wall-sized cabinet divided into small squares. Since women always had to cover their heads in church, boarders kept their black velour hats in their particular cubical. As I got older, I refused to wear my stupid black hat on the streetcar. Instead I'd use a bobby pin to secure a piece of fresh folded Kleenex to my head, dash into the chapel to say a prayer, and as an excuse to see more, peek into one of the many parlors on the convent side to view an unidentified elderly nun lying between two ferns and a candle. It was that spiral staircase outside of the chapel that always intrigued me the most. It went down into the bowels of the convent. Unless you entered the nunnery upon graduation, no student was allowed to look or go down those stairs.

On some days after school I would climb the wide stairs to the third floor. The seldom used upper level was part of the oldest section of the convent school. A window at each end of the hall produced eerie filtered shards of light. Along the walls were huge dusty mahogany and glass vitrines. Each case contained a variety of stuffed birds or animals, each of which was in a sad state and covered by years with a dusty dandruff. On that same floor was an unused, very large Victorian art studio with huge wooden easels and a number of plaster busts. Tucked in between the cases at the other end of the hall was a small room where a lay person taught a few students elocution lessons privately after school hours. I would stand behind the door in the hall, listening how to enunciate and project the voice. Although I didn't realize it at the time, each visit to the third floor was imprinted in my psyche, only to surface many years later.

The same was true of the heavenly golden harp hidden behind the wine velvet curtains on the stage of the old auditorium. From time to time I would visit that beautiful instrument and wonder why was it there, was it ever played, and who could play it? I wished I could.

On some days my mother did not pack my lunch, but instead, tied a dime into the corner of my white cotton hanky so I could buy my lunch. I bought my lunch in the refectory, a place where the resident students took their meals and where there were many, many more rules. Number one rule was no talking, which was almost impossible for me. Second was the fact that you had to eat everything on your plate, even "squaaash". The name alone turned me off.

After you entered the long dark dining room you promptly took a vacant seat. The tables were set for ten from the previous meal. At the sound of the high-pitched dinner bell, you would take your plate off of the table, walk to the back of the hall, and stick your plate through an eight by eight opening. On the other side, a young novice or postulant, (you could never see her face just her hands) would fill your plate. You returned to your seat in silence to eat and hear a nun reading about the unhappy and difficult life of a saint. There was always another nun who walked with her hands tucked into her wide sleeves. She moved in and out from between the tables floating like a silent black angel making sure that you sat up straight and that you were paying attention to the story. If you slouched, she was right there behind you, one hand would come out from beneath that sleeve, and her thumb would dig up and down your spine.

When the meal was finished, one student from each table returned to the back to fetch a white enamel pan of soapy hot water with a small white cotton mop resting in the water. This was returned to the table where the girl at the head of the table washed, another dried and one reset the table for the next meal. The pan with the dirty water was returned to the back. After each meal the girls shifted one seat over, replacing the girl at the head of the table. I knew then that I could never be a nun!

I went to school there and never lost my fascination for those buildings and their contents. Hardwood, marble, and terrazzo floors were always gleaming. Nothing could be spilled on those floors. I spent a lot of time on my hands and knees with a handful of steel wool cleaning spills from my bottle of ink. The good sisters were training us to be young ladies, and running was never allowed. I was always caught and scolded.

My misdeeds were all very innocent, but it seemed that out-of-the-ordinary things only happened to me. I was in second grade when my class had a Christmas party. Everyone sat at their desk with an open paper napkin, a "serviette", and a paper cup in front of them. Sister bent down on one knee to open the red cream soda that I brought for the party. The bottle exploded, leaving the good Sister looking like a bright Flamingo with soda dripping down from her beak. Her white, starched linen wimple and bib immediately turned the color of a red spring rose.

Raising her dripping self up off of the floor she screamed, "Who brought the cream soda?" Of course, it was me, who had innocently jiggled it all the way to school on the crowded street car.

Since I skipped third grade, nothing untoward happened, but in fourth grade I participated in a spelling bee. A few girls, including myself, were lined up against the large silver steam radiator. As the girls were eliminated, they took their seat. I was one of the three remaining contestants, and I stood there with my hands behind my back. The bell rang for recess just as I heard something fall off of the radiator. Everyone, including myself, left the classroom. When we returned after thirty minutes, the classroom door was opened and the air inside was white with hot steam. I had knocked off the steam vent with my nervous twitching fingers. We couldn't use that classroom for the rest of the day.

I have admitted that silence was a very difficult thing for me. I wanted to share all of my exciting adventures with anyone who would listen. There were three punishments for talking during class and I experienced all of them. A teacher could have you kneel facing the blackboard, with both arms extended for a given period of time.

The second I hated. The teacher's desk was built with a chastity panel that faced the students and did not expose the good sister's ankles. This formed a dark cubby hole that was opened on the chair side. Talkative students like me were shoved into that space on the floor. The teacher would then sit and advance her chair into the space and fluff up yards of her black cloth skirt. And there you were underneath, crunched up and hardly breathing. The length of time spent under the desk depended on the severity of the crime and/or the teacher's mood. The worst punishment was to be sent to the office for the rubber strap. That only happened to me once. I remember that the principal, Sister Saint Stephen, began to cry at the thought of inflicting pain on me. I was so fascinated to see her cry that I couldn't cry myself.

Seventh grade was the worst! My teacher was Sister Saint Louis and there was no pleasing her and certainly no chemistry between us. She must have been born just plain mean and nasty. I spent a lot of time among her skirts underneath her desk. My upper arms were often black and blue from her grabbing me, then hauling me out of my seat. I would show my mother my arms, but she offered no comfort. I couldn't wait for that year to end.

I was so excited to begin my first day of high school, which was grade nine. The school had mailed my new room number. There, sitting at the front desk was Sister Saint Louis, who would now be my home room teacher. I wanted to kill myself. When I got home that night, I tearfully begged my mother to call the school and request another classroom. She refused because, after all, it was only for a year, but I felt it would be an eternity. And it was.

Every spring on March 19, the school celebrated the feast of Saint Joseph. Students were allowed to wear "civies" for the day. I decided to sew my first dress. My mother gave me money for a pattern, material and the use of our old Singer treadle sewing machine. I selected a very plain and classic pattern, and the newest thing in material called wool jersey. I worked hard on that dress and was proud of the results. The morning I wore it to school, Sister Saint Louis called me to the front of the classroom. She told my classmates that this dress was not modest. She bent sideways to reach deep into her side pocket. She pulled out what looked like a big blanket pin. With one hand she gathered up the material surrounding my neck, almost chocking me, while the other hand pierced the new fabric with the thick pin.

"Jacqueline" she said, "do not remove this pin while you are in this school".

At lunch time, when I should have felt so proud of something that I had made, I felt awful in front of all of the other students. Again, my mother Blanche took no action. If you look hard, there is always a positive to every negative event. I found out that I loved to sew and that I was pretty good at it.

Each of my report cards reported a need to improve my deportment and application, information my mother completely ignored. My marks were awful. I don't think my father ever saw one of my report cards. He was either working or sleeping.

After twelve years at Saint Joseph's College School, I graduated, without any honours, in 1952.

# CABBAGETOWN

Our home on Naismith in Toronto's Cabbagetown was one of twelve semi-detached houses on each side of the street, making a total of forty-eight homes. Each double house was separated from the next by a narrow dirt path, just wide enough for a Model T car, but none of the residents had one. On one side of each house there was a square opening for the coal shoot. The coal man, always grimy and covered with black coal dust, could dump his bag of coal into each basement. Each double house had a very small six by six porch in the back, divided by a high wooden partition. My father nailed a sturdy wooden orange crate on our side of our plank wood battleship gray divider. As soon as the weather got cold enough, we would store food outdoors. It was wartime and meat was rationed. Even though my father was a butcher, my mother had to save her meat coupons for the Christmas turkey, which was bought and then stored in that outdoor orange crate. It turned out to be a sad holiday in 1943 because when she went to retrieve the bird to put it in the oven, the long-awaited celebratory fowl had been stolen off of the porch.

All of the spaces inside our house were small. My mother converted the parlor into a bedroom, which was separated from the dining room by a wooden pocket door. The dining room then became the living room. The kitchen was no nonsense and utilitarian. There was a basic white enamel electric stove and an ice box. For those who don't know, an ice box was a wooden cabinet that did not require electricity. It had three parts, a lid that opened up on the top and contained a hunk of ice, the middle with shelves to store your food, and a bottom panel that flipped up from the front. Under this panel was an enamel catch pan that caught the melted ice water and required nerves of steel when lifting and emptying it. It always spilled! Ice was sold by the pound. For delivery purposes, Blanche would put a card in the front window turned to the 25-pound side. The delivery man, with huge ice tongs, delivered your ice from his truck and dropped it into the upper tin section of the box with a loud thud. The iceman could be very special to kids playing on the street. With one thrust of his ice pick, he would chip off a big hunk of ice then wrap it newspaper, and hand it to you with a smile. Specks of dirt from the road or sawdust from the bottom of the truck never mattered. The ice was pure magic on a hot summer day.

At that time, newspapers were magic too. They had so many uses, and only cost pennies. Most people, but not my family, read the newspaper for the news itself, but there was so much more. Newspaper could be wrapped around a block of ice to slow down the melt, and a half sheet was the perfect size for a neighbourhood store to wrap a batch of hot fish and chips. Newspapers could be partnered with a cheap bottle of ammonia to clean all surfaces, especially windows. My mother used a fully opened section to put in the windows on a hot day for instant cooling. Shred it and you have garden mulch. Spread it out and it could be used for any medical emergency or for home childbirth. Newer immigrants preferred having their baby at home.

Every spring my mother and I walked the few blocks to the 5 & 10 cent store on Parliament Street to survey the newly arrived bolts of colorful oilcloth. She would select a new pattern for the wooden kitchen table and that was the extent of her home décor. There was always a calendar on the depressing hospital green kitchen walls. The rest of the house had no pictures, bric-a-brac, flowers, magazines, and only a few newspapers and two books. One was a big red book about manners written by Munroe Leaf called "How To Behave and Why". The second was a bed-time story book with 365 pages, a page for each night of the year. When I learned to read, I could read myself a story. What I really liked were comic books, loaned to me by my neighbour Owen McBride, who became a Trappist monk in Texas.

Upstairs were three very small bedrooms and a very small community bathroom. I use the word community because she now began to take in boarders, something she did for the many years to follow.

Growing up in Cabbagetown in the 1940's was wonderful. Families from Eastern and Southern Europe came with many cultural and religious backgrounds. They had survived the Great Depression and were considered by other Torontonians as the working poor. Ambitious immigrants in our neighbourhood, mostly Macedonian and Greek, were getting a foothold in their new country. Catholic French-Canadian residents were not accepted by many.

The neighbourhood had the typical sights and sounds of the day. Milk, fruits and vegetables, ice, and coal were all delivered. The knife sharpener and the ragman called out as they went from street to street and alley to alley and stopped upon request. A few blocks west of my house there was a green grocer, a Scottish bakery, a 5 & 10 cent store, a bank and two theatres. A Saturday afternoon matinee was a must for all of the kids in the neighbourhood, and if you attended in the evening you could bring home a piece of colorful china or flatware.

To the north and east at the edge of the neighbourhood was the Toronto Zoo, St. James Cemetery with its wonderful cemetery art, and the Don Valley with its river and rolling hills, each place a perfect playground for a young solitary visitor. On most of my summer excursions I would disappear for the day, having great conversations and asking pertinent questions of the zookeepers, the animals themselves, the cemetery caretaker and the blessed buried souls lying under all of that interesting artwork. Nobody at home ever seemed to miss me.

***

When I had children of my own, I often thought back to a particular very vivid memory, something that happened when I was eight years old. I always came home from school to an empty house since my parents and our lodgers were at work until dinner time. I guess I was an original "latch key" kid. In the winter months the unspoken rule was that all children were expected to be in the house by dark. One day I returned home from school on a cold late winter afternoon. I was bored. I thought up an impulsive adventure, a habit that I continued to practice my entire life! I dressed myself in snow gear and dragged my sleigh more than a half hour distance, walking to the edge of the neighbourhood, down three big hills, across the ravine and the Don River, and then up three more hills to the far side of the Don Valley. By now it was pitch dark and not a soul was anywhere. I looked down back into the valley from the east side. It was so quiet. I was so high I could see the lamplights below on the bridge that crossed the Don River and far, far ahead, the street lights of Cabbagetown. I was so alone. I sat on my sleigh at the top of the highest hill, tightly grabbed the rope that steered the sled rudder, put my feet up and began my trip down to the bottom.

Halfway down I hit a tree. The metal runner snapped apart and gored me through my snow pant leg, and then into my skin. Yeow, it hurt. I was frightened. and I started to cry but no one could hear me. I was so cold. The tears and snot froze to my face, and I knew I had to get home. I dragged that sleigh all the way back home. I practically fell through the door of my house. Everyone was eating at the table. My mother said casually "where were you?" No angst or search parties. I really wanted someone to miss me. I wanted someone to hug me. I still have the scar on my upper left leg. This memory always prompted me to give my own children an extra hug.

Centered in my neighbourhood were three small groups of individuals who were very different than my family, and who made a lifelong impression. Three blocks away on Carleton Street, a family from Bath, England, lived in a big white Victorian house, one of the largest houses in the neighbourhood. I became friends with their daughters Carole and her sister Nanette Angell. I adored going into their home. Mrs. Angell had her personal touches everywhere. With long high windows, the rooms were always flooded with light, so different from our gloomy house. The walls were painted white, and green ferns in shiny brass containers mixed in between the dark mahogany furniture. All the brass pieces were polished every Saturday morning. Imagine, they had an upright piano, and it too, was painted white. The round padded piano stool was covered with material that was trimmed with a circle of embroidered silk pink rosettes and aqua green leaves. There were many other handcrafted accessories, all colored in the softest pastels. Mrs. Angell often invited me to dinner, where the table was set in true British tradition, introducing me to table settings, Yorkshire Pudding and Lemon Tarts. She instilled in me my love of light and space. She taught me how important it is to make your surroundings, no matter how little you have, a special place of calm and respite for your family and for those who enter. It didn't have to do with money, it had to do with imagination and creativity.

When I was eight years old Carole, Nanette, and I gathered as many used goods as we could carry to the corner of Carleton and Parliament Streets. Parents didn't help you haul in those days. We made tables out of three orange crate boxes, played George Formby records on an old Victrola to attract customers, and sold $7.31 worth of "stuff" for the Evening Telegram British War Victims' Fund. A photographer from the newspaper came and took our pictures. That was my first bit of press. Much more followed during my future years.

Another friend, Shirley Hoffman, lived in an apartment building nearby. Her family had fled Nazi Austria just before the war. From time to time I was invited to visit. Her father Karl, his spectacles perched on the end of his nose, always sat in front of an easel, painting mountain and lake scenes of his native country. Classical and operatic music played in the background. I soaked in that new and exciting environment. I would dwell on those scenes, uplifted by the background music, and wished that someday I would travel to those very places, far from my neighbourhood. And I did. Rose and Karl Hoffman began my life-long love of classical music, art, faraway places, limburger cheese and herring. I only wish I had known enough to ask them how the war had impacted their lives. The Hoffman family certainly impacted mine.

Across the dirt divide of our house and our next-door neighbors on Naismith Street lived the four Hart sisters. I never knew any of their first names because it was considered impolite for young people to use a first name for an adult. Always Miss, Missus, or Mister. The women were British maiden ladies who came and went in silence, and if you were lucky, one would give you a little nod. Every morning the three Miss Harts walked the few blocks to work at the Warder Box Factory, which specialized in paper jewelry boxes. One Miss Hart stayed home to cook and clean, which was a pretty neat arrangement. If I went down that dirt divide between our houses and looked straight ahead at our backyard, all I could see was more dirt, a lonely Sumac tree close to the porch, and a clothesline. But, when I turned to my right, the Hart yard beckoned with all of the majesty of a fine English manor landscape. It was a traditional English garden from wire fence to wire fence, with one narrow long path down the middle, blue delphiniums, asters, monkshood, roses, and more. Entrance was by invitation only. I would lean on the fence until the gardening sister, known to me only by the name of Miss Hart, would beckon me to come in with a queenly wave. She rarely spoke, but rather worked away as I tagged along behind. I was a gabby little thing, but in that magical garden I just knew not to speak in case I would break the spell. I just watched every single thing she did. In the spring, just at the perfect time, she would bring out small maroon colored jewelry boxes with shiny golden paper lids. The seeds that she had culled in the fall had been carefully stored in the marked boxes would now be planted for three more seasons of color and fruition. I was in love with, and truly happy in that garden. To this day, I have a need to work in a garden for the gifts of beauty and peace.

One of the downsides to our grassless backyard with the solitary Sumac tree was that during the month of May I could never contribute flowers to the class "May Altar", which always put you in good graces with your teacher. On the other hand, the branches from that Sumac tree, when tied together with string, made a neat hula skirt. A blanket hung carefully over the clothes line identified the stage for one of my make-believe plays. Each play ended up with my same signature line, "Madame you are drinking sea water, not tea water".

# A BROTHER PAUL

During the school year, I didn't fit in socially with all of my fellow students from well-heeled neighbourhoods. In my own neighbourhood I was some kind of a lone freak. They wore clothes that looked the same as every kid across Canada at the time. I, on the other hand, looked different. Neighbourhood kids all left and came home from school at the same time. I left earlier than the local kids, and came home later, but I liked that part because I usually had an adventure on the way home. What I didn't like were the clunky black oxford shoes, itchy black wool stockings with generous black bloomers underneath, a black pleated serge uniform topped off by a round brimmed black wool hat which was always secured under my double chin by a thin piece black elastic. That was my mother's insurance in case I lost that expensive hat because I was always in another fabricated and exciting world and always losing things.

I made every trip home from school an adventure. When other students were learning their times tables in class, I was plotting which streets to take, and which downtown establishment I would visit on my way home. I was careful never to repeat a route the following day. One route would take me past the SPCA where I would go in and pretend that I was selecting a pet. Another route took me to the Eaton's College store where I pretended to select a china, or sterling, or crystal pattern for my mother. I liked

Eaton's for another reason. I spent hours wandering the colorful art gallery on the second floor. Nobody ever questioned me or sent me home. On nearby Yonge Street at the Heintzman Piano store and at Capezio, a store for ballet supplies, I selected a new piano and tried on toe shoes for my make-believe ballet class. The amazing thing was that all of the sales people were kind and patient, and went along with this ruse, spending time with me. Today, I'm sure I'd hear "get out of here kid". My very favorite route took me to the Allan Gardens on College Street, a glass botanical garden with many attached greenhouses. I trailed after the gardeners, always asking a ton of questions.

My father was now working at a butcher shop close to my school. My mother had saved her ration stamps to buy an expensive roast of beef, a rare treat during the Second World War. She asked me to go and pick up the roast at my father's shop on my way home from school. My father wrapped the meat in butcher paper and tied the package with twine. I put the twine under my finger and headed for Allan Gardens for a short impromptu visit. Across the street from the greenhouses was a church on the corner. My habit, I'd done it dozens of times, was to hop, yes, I mean hop, up the five church entrance stairs, then jump down behind the double-faced message board, and continue down around the corner towards my home on Naismith Street. The twine was cutting into my finger. I put the package down for a minute. When I got home my mother looked for her package and I admitted that I left it behind the church sign. I ran back those many blocks, but alas, it was gone. I just know that some dog really enjoyed it.

Just down the street on that favorite route was the wallpaper store. I'd sit on the high chair behind the tall counter flipping the large pages, absorbing all of the colors and designs. One day the owner asked me if I wanted to take a book home and keep it because new books were coming in. Of course, I said yes! After a few days I figured out how to make a wallet out of one folded colorful page, all put together with flour and water paste. Those wallets became my gift to anyone who would take them. It was also an entree into interesting conversation. I returned from time to time for other out-of-date sample books. My father was right. Just like the song, the best things in life were free, and all you needed was a little imagination!

My mother gave me money to take out a membership at the YWCA on Gerrard Street at Yonge located next door to where my father worked. I made this stop whenever the spirit moved me since no one was ever waiting for me at home. The "Y" supplied faded once navy cotton regulation one-piece bathing suits and towels. There was never anyone in the pool in the late afternoon hours. The pool was wonderful, but the hot showers were divine. And they had hair dryers set into the walls. The YWCA would continue in many ways to weave itself into many future events of my life.

1945 was important for me many ways. I had never seen my mother cry. I came home from school one day in early April only to find my mother weeping with a Life magazine on her lap. On the cover was a large picture of President Franklin Delano Roosevelt who had died on April 12. I never saw her cry again.

Three weeks later, on May 8, church bells rang, horns blared, and people cheered as they celebrated VE Day, or Victory in Europe. The school was abruptly closed that morning, and I remember walking home in the glorious warm spring sunshine, listening to the beeping car horns and experiencing the happiness of unknown strangers who waved at me as I passed them on the street.

***

Our first boarder on Naismith Street was my Uncle Rheal. At 29 years old, my mother's brother came to Toronto from Quebec to look for work. He found a job as a handyman for a four-story apartment building a few blocks away. He was handsome and extremely nervous and timid, a man who rode his bicycle to work every day, always wrapping his pant cuffs with metal clips to prevent an accident. I remember that he was afraid to ride his bicycle in the rain. He had stayed with us for almost a year, when one cold January day in 1942, a police officer appeared at our door. It seems that Rheal was leaning into the elevator pit to make a repair in the basement of the building, when the elevator came all the way down and took off his head.

The next boarder to live with us was a chef by the name as Gerry Gamache. He adored my mother who, unlike the restaurant staff and patrons where he worked, could speak to him in French. His room was so small, just room enough for a single bed, a straight chair and a dresser. As strange as this may seem, he had a penchant for knitting argyle socks. He left the door open most of the time, I'm sure to circulate the air. I remember him sitting in that chair, manipulating yellow bobbins of different colors wools which hung down from three knitting needles. The finished products were argyle socks and were always donated to the British War Victims Fund. He never married, and looking back, I suppose he was gay, but back then gender preference was an unspoken subject. He acted ambivalent towards me. I was just there. Life for him was all about his beautiful best friend, Blanche. That friendship would pay off at a later date.

After Rheal died his room became available, after which a long succession of single French-Canadian girls came, each staying for a period of about six months. I especially remember Adeline Smith who had a mysterious locked mahogany hope chest at the foot of her bed and was constantly knitting baby clothes. At my age I never questioned their circumstances.

The last female boarder I remember at our house on Naismith Avenue was my mother's cousin from St. George de Beauce. She left Naismith Street about six months later in the same week that my brother was born. On April 16, 1946, my mother at age 38, gave birth to a healthy, chubby baby boy named Paul Raymond. I was not an only child any more.

In those days new mothers stayed in the hospital to rest and recuperate for eight days. In St. Michael's Hospital that same week in April were my mother and her baby boy Paul, her dear friend and cousin Cecile Waters holding her baby boy Ronald, and her sister Laureda. Laureda had come to Toronto to take care of me, but she stepped on a rusty nail while chopping wood for the furnace and was also hospitalized. Another of my mother's cousins from Quebec delivered her baby boy in that same week. His name I will never know.

My mother added a crib for Paul in the downstairs front bedroom, which was formerly a living room. When Paul was about three months old, she put him in his crib for his afternoon nap and left me to watch him for a short time. I sat in the summer sunshine on the top of our chipped grey five front steps, taking in the world. There were not many cars in our neighbourhood so I was startled to see a car zoom to a sudden stop next to the curb, only a short distance in front of me. A man jumped out of his car, clearing the running board. He left the engine running.

He rushed past me yelling, “I’m getting my kid”.

He entered the front hall, saw the crib in the room to his right and tried to grab the baby. I grabbed him and started screaming. Our next door neighbour Mr. Bourdon heard me and came running into our front hall. The man dropped Paul back into the crib, ran back to his car and took off. It seemed that the man was the father of Blanche’s cousin’s baby, and he thought that Paul belonged to him. Afterwards no one knew how the man got our address, but it was all very, very exciting.

***

In the summer, out of the blue, my mother, without explanation, said she was sending me to my Aunt Laureda’s cottage located just north of Montreal. She packed a small bag for me, put a butcher twine necklace with my vital information around my neck, and took me to the Union Station. I was ten years old. She introduced me to the Station Master. I was so excited for this impromptu and sudden adventure on the train. Little did I know how this trip would impact my future. I wasn't told at the time why there was such a rush to "remove me from the scene".

This story is believable until this point, but the following really happened this way. My aunt and her son Bobby, four years younger than I, met me at the train station, then took a cab to her cottage.

The next morning after I arrived my aunt had an idea. She suggested that the three of us go outside and begin a game of leap frog. Very strange. It was still early in the day and there was heavy moisture on the grass. It was my turn to put my hands on my thighs and bend over. A generous sized Aunt Laureda leaped over me and slipped in that morning dew. I collapsed. She grabbed my two shoulders and shook me, telling me to get up. I was crying and in great pain, and it was obvious that I had broken something. This part is really unbelievable. She called her favorite cab company. While I waited, she went into the cottage to get two pillows and that butcher twine ID necklace. When the cab pulled up, she put my information back around my neck, put me into the back seat of the cab with the pillows under my elbows, and told the driver to take me to Montreal General emergency room. I wasn't excited any more, I felt that recurring feeling of being frightened and all alone.

I had broken my right collarbone. The doctors applied a heavy plaster cast from my neck down to my waist, and down my entire right arm. Then they sent me to the children's ward. That night I called the nurse to tell her that I had blood on the inside of my upper leg. She explained that I was now a young lady, and this was going to happen every month for a very long time. I was confused. I needed someone to hug me...

After two weeks with no news from my aunt, mother or father, a nurse took me to the side door of the hospital where my aunt and a cab were waiting to take me back to the train station.

When I arrived back in Toronto, my mother gave me startling news. I was not going home to Naismith Avenue. She explained to me what had happened.

It seems that my parents rented their house from a Macedonian family who now wanted to occupy the house that they owned. My parents had no resources to just pick up and move and had refused to leave. The Sheriff came and moved their goods, along with the occupants, onto the sidewalks of Naismith. That must have been an ugly scene. To the rescue came Jerry Gamache, my mother's faithful friend, who must have had money in one of those argyle socks he was always knitting. He bankrolled my parents, really my mother, to buy a rather large house in another part of Toronto's east end. The house had been the office and residence of a doctor who was retiring, a house where there would be lots of rooms to rent. God love him.

At ten years old I found this hard to understand. I was going to a new house in a different neighbourhood. I was shocked and sad. I hadn't had a chance to say goodbye to any of my friends, including Carole, Shirley, and Owen. Now I couldn't have any more adventures on my walk home from school because my new house was too far away. Because of the distance, I had to take the streetcar home. There was also that baby brother who was getting all of the attention.

A month later my mother and I descended into the bowels of the Hospital for Sick Children to receive care at the Public Clinic in order to have my heavy cast removed. The narrow halls had low ceilings covered with hissing pipes, with an occasional bench lined along the wall. The air was stifling because of the steam pipes. We sat there for a very long time, and finally a stranger removed the cast, after which my mother and I climbed back up the steep stairs to the blinding daylight, then took the street car back to my new home. Maybe that's why I now freak out in tight dark spaces.

# THE NEW NEIGHBOURHOOD

The new house sat next to the Gerrard Street streetcar tracks. Every few minutes, in both directions, a red and cream TTC car would clank by our block-long row of houses. Riverdale Collegiate was directly across the street, taking up the whole block. Everything seemed very different. My mother organized the spaces in the house, maximizing possible space for boarders. This time the dining room became my parents' bedroom. Over time, a parade of people came and went from the upstairs, and given my active imagination, it seemed to me that each person had a secret. Blanche was always tight lipped about their backgrounds. The string of single young women who stayed about six months continued. My mother's artistic young cousin Ludovic, four years older than I, came to stay. He was an artistic homosexual who wore extremely heavy orange pancake makeup and spoke with an affected British/French accent. That was a real eye opener for an innocent thirteen-year old convent girl.

Blanches' group of boarders was always eclectic and interesting to an observant young girl. We harbored a handsome IRA leader Maurice Lynch who had thick black curly hair, very blue eyes, a thick brogue and who was wanted by the law in Ireland. He had an affair with Sophie, the Polish business woman who had black hair with a red sheen, coal black eyes and one severe and drab brown suit. She thought she was a princess and occupied the bedroom next to Maurice. One minute they were in love, but the next minute tempers flared, black eyes flashed, and they were screaming at each other. One time, Sophie hit Maurice over the head with the telephone receiver and broke the receiver in half. The repairman from Bell Canada said he had worked for Bell Canada over many years and it was the first time he had ever seen a receiver broken in half. I'll bet Maurice had a headache after that knock on the head. My mother enjoyed female boarders the best, less trouble she said, and so there was a string of lovely college students from Ryerson University, one of whom made my long white graduation dress. My bedroom was never really mine. It changed from time to time if my mother deemed it necessary. I was never asked.

***

After moving into this new house, my father seemed to completely disappear from view. He had taken a job with the CPR Railroad, which required him to work from late afternoon until after midnight. When I left in the morning he was sleeping and when I came home after school he was gone. He worked at a butcher shop all day Saturday in Thornhill, Ontario, which was a long drive in his used Ford, a car he was very proud of. When I did see him, he looked stooped, tired and defeated. It seemed that all he did was work to keep my mother Blanche happy. There was no joy left in his life and not much to sing about. He had a beautiful voice as did my brother Paul. People thought that my voice was very pleasant too. In school I looked forward to our weekly chorale class taught by well-known Canadian composer and Music Educator Godfrey Ridout. My grandson Frank has inherited celestial vocal cords and in college he sang with the college choir. I hope that when he becomes a working man, he will join another choir because singing is so good for the soul. My son Tom told me once that when he looks back to his childhood, he remembers his mother (me) always singing around the house. That's so much better than remembering a screaming mother!

The local parish church was St. Joseph's Church, not to be confused with the name of my school downtown. During mass I would listen to the choir and later asked the Director if I could join the group, in spite of the fact that choir members all went to the local parish school. She said yes. The choir led to a teen friendship with Joan Sartor, a girl who was my age and who lived just around the corner from my new house. Every Sunday morning, I sang at two masses. I sang in the parish choir and then took the streetcar to sing noon mass at St. Anne's just two streetcar stops away. I'm proud to say that I learned how to chant from the Latin Gregorian hymnal. Singing in church has always seemed to me to be such a pure experience.

My new friend Joan's mother, who came from Finland, was a bit of a thing and was bedridden. She looked like a small pea lost in a pod of bedcovers. Her Italian father, Tony Sartor, was the first in his family to immigrate to Canada. Most of his family still lived in Italy and the reunification of his family in Canada was his first priority. Although unschooled in urban ways, he bought his small detached house in our residential working-class neighbourhood. A plus for him was that it was located close to a major public transportation line. His trade was bricklaying. He sponsored his two brothers and finally a sister-in-law to live in Canada. They all lived crowded together and everyone pooled their resources to form a social and economic network. They gave each other emotional strength in a new country.

Toronto in 1947 had become a booming and changing urban centre, with a shortage of labourers for an ever-expanding community. Canada lifted its restrictions against the admission of Italians, recently barred as former enemy aliens. Great numbers of Italians came by boat train from Montreal, pouring into the Toronto Union Station. There were plenty of work opportunities for the new arrivals, especially in the construction business. Canadian legislation against Asians remained in place however and administrative tinkering assured that Southern and Eastern Europeans, especially Jews, would now find it difficult to get into Canada.

Every day Joan would hurry home from the local school to cook dinner and sometimes I would go over to help her. It was drudge work to her, but it was all too fascinating for me. The men would arrive from work and immediately plunk down at the kitchen table and pour themselves a glass of vino rosso from the two already filled glass pitchers on the table. The Sartors were from the area north of Rome, tall and handsome muscular men with reddish blond hair. They were all dressed alike, dusty beige work pants, heavy dusty work boots, and on the top, a white muscle shirt with copious amounts of hair spilling from under their armpits. Sometimes they came to the table with a white handkerchief still molded over their head, each corner tied in a knot. They were always loud, laughing one minute and then yelling with hand gestures in the next breath. And always in Italian. The meals were very basic and economical, pasta, sauce, and large loaves of Italian bread that were never sliced. The men just pulled it apart to soak up the sauce and then wash it down with more red wine. I loved that scene because it was so lively and so different than at my house where no one had much in common, and where it was always quiet and subdued.

One evening Joan called me to say that her mother was really sick with pneumonia and that she was too exhausted to sit up with mother for another night. She needed a night's sleep. I walked around the corner to her house around 11:00 p.m. Since the men of the house got up very early to work construction, everyone was already in bed. She shut out all of the lights except for a dim hall light.

The light cast an eerie shadow just past the open door of her mother's bedroom. Joan went to bed in her own room. I entered her mother's room, pulled up a straight chair and placed it into the shadow near the head of her bed. I took out my rosary and started to pray. All I could hear was her mother's laboured breathing. A bit after midnight the steady cadence of her breathing stopped. She started to choke on her phlegm. I put my arm around her neck and moved her forward to spit. Then there was a deep guttural sound, and then nothing but silence. She had died in my arms. I don't know why but I didn't scream, I was very calm. I knocked on Joan's bedroom door to tell her that her mother was gone. This event would not be the only time that I would have an intimate meeting with death. In each case the memories are vivid.

There must have been an underground information network among the new Italian community in Toronto. There were seventy-five cars in the funeral cortege. Most who participated didn't even know the deceased, but they came out in a community to support their fellow Italian immigrant Tony Sartor. During my high school years Joan slowly disappeared from my life.

***

One day I stayed on the streetcar one extra stop to check out the local neighbourhood YWCA. A list of their programs included a class in Modern Dance. The class stressed the philosophy of the brilliant Isadora Duncan and the American dance movement, "let them come forth with great strides, leaps and bounds, with lifted forehead and far-spread arms, to dance." I loved the idea of dancing in my bare feet and wearing a long flowing Grecian dress of navy crepe. I signed up on the spot. I met some really nice girls who took the class with me. They all already knew each other because they were sorority sisters who went to Riverdale Collegiate, the high school across the street from my new house. The girls were so friendly that I soon joined them at the "Y" teen club.

At one meeting the group decided to have an ecumenical meeting at the nearby United Church. During the planning they asked me if I would attend and give a homily on 'One God' since I was the only Roman Catholic. Never short of words and an opinion, I agreed. A few days after I gave my homily, I was called to the school office. The word was out at school about my transgression to the Catholic faith. To make things worse, they knew that I had taken out a "Y" membership. I would surely burn in the fires of hell.

The next September I was invited to be a pledge for my new friends' sorority, the first non-Riverdale girl to be asked to join their ranks. There were five chapters of the sorority, two in Toronto, one in St. Catherines, one in Niagara Falls, Ontario and one in Niagara Falls, New York.

***

Except for Botany and Zoology school was a total bore. I just was not interested in school. My courses were designed for that group of students that were planning to go to college or be a nun or a nurse. I wasn't interested in any of that, but I thought that I might become a Physical Education teacher since I was quite a good athlete. Basketball and swimming were my best sports. I never had even one conversation with either of my parents about school and they never asked what I wanted to do with my life. I guess they thought the good sisters were taking care of all such matters. Or maybe they were just too busy or tired to care.

# THE AMAZING REUNION

I needed a Saturday and holiday job for a number of reasons, but especially because I wanted to have a bit of spending money and perhaps enough to buy an obligatory hope chest, something almost every teenage girl had to have.

My first job was at Christmas for a two-week stint at Woolworths on the corner of Yonge and Queen Streets on the very spot where Eaton Center and the subway entrance now stands. I put red, green and white tissue paper in a bundle and then wrapped each roll with a cardboard circle. I hated it!

Shortly after, I found an ad in the newspaper from someone in need of a part-time person to do light housekeeping, which was a joke because I didn't do a thing at home, not even boil water. I answered the ad and hopped onto a streetcar for a ride to the Spadina area, which was a predominantly Jewish neighbourhood. The homeowner told me that she kept an orthodox/kosher kitchen and that it was important to keep dairy items and meat items separate. I only lasted three days, but I chalked it up to a new life-skill. I learned a good bit about the food and customs of a Jewish household in a very short time. I absorbed even the briefest happening in my life for use at a later time. I was like a sponge.

The next summer I decided to pick strawberries. I lasted one day longer than my housekeeping job. I took the streetcar to the end of the east end line. A long way. From there an open-bed truck transported the workers to a farm, where everyone scrambled to fill as many quart baskets as they could, since your pay depended how many baskets you filled. I worked slower than the others because I only filled my baskets with perfect, red luscious berry, avoiding strawberries with a blemish or not fully ripe. At the end of the first day the skin on my back between my shorts and my blouse was burned to the color of one of those perfect red berries. My life lesson in that brief job was God bless the workers in the field. I guessed I would never save enough for a hope chest.

Zuccero's green grocery was located on Leslie Street, just around the corner from our house. The family had built an extension onto the front of their house which had become a store filled with Italian food items. Outside fresh fruits and vegetables were displayed from orange crates carefully placed on the sidewalk. They were always busy because of the quality of their products and they delivered groceries too. I asked if I could work there after school and on Saturdays. I asked myself "how hard this could be?" Mama Zuccero sat in the very back of the store on a straight chair surveying every aspect of the business like a mother hawk. She was always dressed in black. Her seven sons all worked in the business. My job was to fill phone orders and get the order ready for delivery, including the total cost. Those boys never used an adding machine, they used a sharpened #2 pencil. As I found each item on the list, I was expected to write the cost of each item in a row on the outside of a brown paper bag, then add them up. I was so slow, and I kept losing my place in the column. At the time I was rotten at math and especially when I was under pressure. It took me forever to add up each column of figures, but it didn't take forever for Mama Zuccero to blow me in because she didn't miss a thing. My take away lesson was a solid knowledge of math and Italian produce and food stuff.

Next, I looked for a job just four doors down the street from my house on Gerrard Street. Miss Carrie Clifford had a china shop and each September she added to her bank book by selling school books to the students of Riverdale Collegiate located just across the street. Now this I could do. I loved the unique smell of the new school books and supplies, plus the china shop nurtured my everlasting love for beautiful English china. I loved that little shop, but Miss Clifford paid a pittance. I continued to look for another opportunity

That fall I applied to Simpson's department store. The building, located on the south side of Yonge and Queen Streets was huge, having ten stories, and taking up one enormous block of downtown Toronto real estate. At the employment office I told the lady I was seventeen. After some questioning, the woman who interviewed me felt that I was better suited to work in the offices of the credit department instead of a sales girl. I then took the nearest elevator to the seventh floor and the newly formed Revolving Credit department. An attractive white-haired woman approached me from in between the long rows of grey metal file cabinets and stared very hard at me. She did not introduce herself, she just continued to stare.

Then she said without looking at my name, "little Jacqueline, I just knew you'd come back into my life".

It was Margaret Johnson, my Preventorium nurse and pseudo mother. What were the chances of "Johnnie" ever finding me again? Amazing. We remained very close friends until she passed away many years later.

***

A Canadian man by the name of Gordon Wright had a life-long philosophy of developing leadership and organizational skills through sports.

He said, "Winning is great, but passing on skills and knowledge so others can be winners is even better."

He established the Ontario Athletic Leadership Camp. Male and female student athletes were selected from every high school in Ontario to receive this award. In grade 12 (at that time in Canada there were 13 grades), I received this leadership honour representing my school. That summer I was sent to Lake Couchiching, north of Orillia, Ontario, to receive intensive training from early morning until dusk, in all of the sports, including archery, volleyball, and canoeing. In return I had to pledge that I would give my services to a non-profit agency for two weeks in the following year. The following summer I took a job as a lifeguard at the Toronto North York pool, and gave classes to Down Syndrome children who adored being in the water.

The OALC camp was great fun, and I established many friendships in the short two weeks that I was there. I met a girl by the name of Nancy Weir, who became my very close friend. We were determined to get together when camp was over. In conversation we discovered that we had something else in common because she was a sorority sister in the Niagara Falls, Ontario, chapter.

***

The first weekend in October is the traditional Canadian Thanksgiving weekend. Every year Nancy's school had an annual football game on that weekend and she invited me to come and stay at her house. She had a friend Bud, who had a friend Jim, and the four of us would have a great time. And we did! My date Jim Allen lived in Niagara Falls, Ontario, and worked at his father's milling company in Niagara Falls, New York. He was movie star handsome, a great dresser, Catholic, American, and his parents had class and money. He was four years older than I. When I got home, I waited for him to call. And he did!

I was just beginning grade twelve, which in the United States was what would be considered a student's last year of high school. I was a mature and very attractive young woman, soon to be a sixteen-year old, who looked and acted much like an eighteen-year old.

My American friend Jim Allen began driving the ninety miles to Toronto to visit me on the weekends. He worked until noon on Saturdays, so it was always a short visit and not nearly enough time to really get to know him. In the early '50s there was no pill and the sexual revolution had not yet arrived. Nice girls, especially Catholic girls, who always feared the wrath of God and eternal damnation, saved themselves for sex until after marriage. A few months later, after two deferments Jim went off to Korea.

In the meantime, I continued to work on Saturdays and holidays at Simpsons and had saved enough money at Christmas time to buy my mother a setting for six of matching white china with deep olive trim and a fine gold edge. She had never owned a complete set of good dishes. I visited my mother years later in California and inquired where were the dishes I had worked so hard for.

She said, "doz ol' tings. I true dem away because everybody here has Franciscan Rose".

If a daughter of mine had given them to me, I would have saved them forever.

I also saved enough money to buy my hope chest. Not the standard long coffin cedar chest that was traditionally placed at the end of a bed, but a narrow mahogany highboy chest with a large cedar bottom drawer. I always wanted something a bit different from the rest of the crowd. It sits in my bedroom and I still love it today.

Since I now had my Red Cross papers, the next summer I applied for and got the job as a lifeguard at the East York public pool. There were both male and female lifeguards and I was the youngest. I was sixteen but again I lied about my age. They were a party group who continued their friendships away from the pool.

***

One of the people that I became friends with was much older than I. His name was Jim MacC. He was a handsome twenty-five year old that had fought in France at the tail end of World War II.

He had been married and divorced. In other words, he had been around. I was an innocent.

A group of my fellow workers, including him, decided to rent a cottage in Muskoka for a week-end so I lied to my mother, saying that I was going to a girl friend's cottage. From the minute I left Toronto and headed north, I was an absolute wreck. I sincerely believed that if I slept with my friend, drowned, or was in an auto accident, having lied to my mother, I would burn in hell for all eternity. Why had I come? I explained to him how I felt. From then on, he treated me like a kid sister. I sat on the shore while everyone else swam to a far-away rock to drink beer. I couldn't wait to get home.

***

The next year I graduated from grade 13 and began a job working for the Canadian National Railway as an Information Specialist. That was a fancy term for a shift working person who gave the times of train arrivals, departures and information over the telephone. An Information Specialist would also put together trips and schedules for far away Canadian destinations, which was something that I really enjoyed. Six other people, male and female, were all heavy smokers, and all very much older than me, working together for each shift. It was an AAA job using a train instead of a car or bus. I loved the job but, since I didn't smoke, I hated the heavy smelly haze.

I dated a few young men while Jim was away, especially a brilliant engineering student four years older than me, whose name was Bill. I saw him on a regular basis. A frequent Saturday date with Bill was getting all dressed up, then both of us would take a 30-minute streetcar ride to the romantic Casa Loma after he had already taken a 40-minute ride east to get to my house. We danced to the Big Band sound. In that amazing dimly lit grand ballroom, all of the doors to the castle's long patio were flung open, allowing the dancers to float through the doors to the outside and dance under the stars. Poor Bill had to repeat the two street car rides on his way home, this time to the west.

Later in Bill's life he became a top executive with British American Oil. I was so young, but that fact did not deter him from telling me that he wanted me to marry him when he finished college. Both Bill and his parents were against the Catholic faith which sent me a tall red flag.

I was eighteen years old when Jim came home in June. He gave me a diamond ring and I began to fill my hope chest with sheets and towels and make plans for a September wedding. It was time to say goodbye to Bill and he was devastated. Ten years later he telephoned me from Toronto to see if my marriage was intact. I said it was, and he was disappointed for a second time.

Jim had been in Korea for fourteen months, which would lead one to think that when he returned home, he would be sexually motivated, and although my hormones were raging, that was not the case for him. When he visited me, he had a very passive attitude towards showing me any sign of affection. He was always quiet, pleasant, kind and oh, so handsome. He told me that he really wanted to get married because, as a devout Catholic, he wanted to fulfill his duty to God and produce children. I was young and unsophisticated. I believed him. Blanche swooned at the thought of her daughter marrying a “reesh” and handsome American. For her, the Catholic part was neither here nor there. She also thought that his ears were perfect, small and flat, and that was something she deemed an important aspect in both babies and adults! Now, from time to time, I find myself checking out ears.

# MARRIAGE AND MOTHERHOOD

That summer I took the train to Niagara Falls, New York, to meet his mother and father. It didn't take long to see that his family was very much different from mine. Jim was a third-generation member of a very successful Western New York company called Allen Milling Company. His mother was a member of the Bampfield family, an important part of the history and wealth of Niagara Falls, Ontario. His parents were formal, decorous, and serious. At our first meeting I was immediately afraid of his father Max, who was a huge, cigar-smoking man who looked just like the actor Charles Coburn. Although their house was very small, everything in it was elegant. It housed Jim's maternal grandmother's beautiful antiques, fine crystal glasses, Wedgwood china and sterling silver. The bed linens were perfectly done at the laundry with a wee bit of starch, making getting into bed every night a hotel experience. Back at my house, for most of my life the dinnerware and silverware were theater giveaways from during the war, we drank out of unmatched empty jelly glasses, and our laundry was hung off of the back porch clothes line to dry. It was like "upstairs/downstairs". There I was, going to be a participant in the upstairs part of society. I did not have many story books growing up. I guess I was making up my own fairy tale. In looking back, I realize that I was in love with the "glamour" of it all, and not really in love with the handsome prince.

***

I went back home to begin to make the wedding arrangements. I had saved every penny from my job and put the money into an account at the neighbourhood Royal Bank. I've always had a very practical streak in me so in pondering the wedding, and since I was paying for it myself, I would have a morning Mass with a luncheon immediately following.

The venue for the lunch was called Fantasy Farms. It was a cottage-like building with beautiful gardens, nestled into the trees of the Don Valley where the Gardiner Expressway now stands. When selecting the menu, I selected the least expensive choice which was chicken salad with garnish and a roll. As far as I was concerned the wedding toast could be done with grape juice instead of wine. My how I've changed! There would be wedding cake and coffee. I saved the top of that wedding cake and used it as a table centerpiece for each of our children's baptisms.

I only tried on one wedding dress. When I saw it displayed in the window of a fashionable Bloor Street shop I splurged. Since I wanted everything simple, my three bridesmaids would wear short dresses and Jim and his groomsmen would dress in grey flannels and navy blazers. His parents did not inquire about any of my arrangements. That would be gauche. They knew the date, the name of the church and my patterns (crystal, china and silver). They would supply a guest list. They would have a dinner for the wedding party the evening before the wedding and pay for flowers as was the tradition.

Jim was back to work for his father. While in Korea he saved all of his pay. The first thing he bought was a shining new 1952 cream colored Pontiac. Jim and his parents looked for a house for Jim and I to begin our life together. No one thought to ask me to come to Niagara Falls just to make sure that I liked whatever they picked as my future home. They selected a three-bedroom house a block around the corner from their house. I was told after the fact. I must admit that I didn't make a fuss, I just went along with it. The word 'obey' was still a part of the marriage vows.

The wedding invitations were out in early August and I had begun to plan my trousseau tea. The 'tea' was a traditional party hosted by the bride's mother usually in the brides' home, with neighbours, colleagues, and acquaintances invited who were not on the formal wedding guest list. On the weekend before the wedding, Blanche laid out my bridal shower and wedding gifts for attendees to admire. The bride's going away clothes, any accessories, and all of the new lacy lingerie including three peignoir sets, white, powder blue and black were on display. I sewed many of my going away outfits, including hats to go with each outfit. Hats were a must.

***

At the same time, my mother Blanche was busy locating her baby sister Helena, whom she had not seen since her sister, then four years old, was being loaded onto a hay wagon. She began by calling a cousin in Lawrence, Massachusetts. She finally located her sister in Santa Monica, California, and an invitation was sent. An invitation was also sent to her sister Laureda in Montreal and her brother Maurice in Quebec City who had bought Mr. McNab's asphalt business upon his patron's retirement. He owned a shiny new black Oldsmobile '98. It was determined that I would go to church in this best family vehicle. Everyone was excited.

***

The weather that Sept. 11 weekend was just perfect. Another 9/11, and there's a message there. On the Friday night, Jim's parents hosted a dinner taking place in Toronto's then luxurious King Edward Hotel. My parents, the bridal wedding party and those who would be attending the wedding from Niagara Falls, New York, were all invited. Wines and top shelf liquor accompanied the superb dinner which seemed even finer served in the elegance of the 'Oak Room'. I wondered, but did not dwell, on how my wedding day arrangements would be received by his family and friends.

***

On Friday my French-Canadian relatives began arriving. When I got home from the dinner that evening, there were wall to wall people all speaking French. My mother had the sofa reupholstered before the many visitors came, so she almost fainted when red wine was spilled on the new material. She tried to put a couple of cousins in my room for the night, but I rebelled. After all, I was the bride! It was very late when everyone finally found a spot to sleep. I was out like a light when, at 2 a.m., I heard a loud crash. The noise level in the house began to rise again. We lived on a main streetcar line, and my uncle Maurice had parked his shining new black Oldsmobile '98 between the streetcar tracks and the curb. A car had plowed into his car. It took a long time for everyone to settle down again. In the morning we rented another car and I was off to the church with my dad.

The wedding mass took place at Saint Joseph's Church. Everything was perfect, especially the weather. At the reception there was a slight breeze blowing through the trees of the Don Valley. In my joy at the time of the reception, I didn't notice that Jim's dad Max was upset and loudly vocal because there was such a skimpy lunch with no wine or liquor. At the end of the reception, I changed into my going away navy suit with a matching hat. I waved goodbye to all of our family and friends. I was now Mary Jacqueline Allen.

***

Immediately following the wedding, we drove to Georgian Bay in Canada. Before entering the United States permanently, it was necessary that I spend three days in Canada before entering the USA. We had rented a cottage on Wasaga Beach on the Canadian side. The beach was devoid of other people since cottage owners, by September, had all closed their properties for the season. The weather was raw with wind and rain. The cold gray waves of Georgian Bay rolled into the shore and hit with a heavy thud. It was 1954 and the non-drinking and virginal couple did not have a clue about romance or lovemaking. Looking back, those three days were really awful and just plain sad.

It was not discussed, just understood, that I would not work. Our new house was on a short street lined with Elm trees, the leaves on each side kissing in the middle. It was interesting that almost all of my new neighbours were members of the temple around the corner, so with a little exaggeration, my unfortunate brief stint in the Jewish section of Toronto made me seem a bit knowledgeable to my new friends.

***

Jim worked in his father's feed store five and a half days a week. Immediately, a daily routine, not to be changed under any circumstance, was established. I served his breakfast at 7:30 a.m. and there was no communication during the day although both of us had access to a telephone. Dinner was to be served at six o'clock on the dot. Jim left the mill at 5:15 p.m., stopping for two quick beers at "Dugers" the local Irish watering hole. The table was set with wedding linen, best dishes and silver. He would bring home the store cash for the day, wrapped in a brown paper bag and secured by a rubber band. For the next twenty-five years it was placed in an indentation on top of the cherry dining room hutch. The set daily routine rarely changed. It would take a big event to be off-schedule. I had just begun to prepare dinner on Thursday, June 7, 1956 when at 5 p.m. the Schoellkopf Power Plant collapsed and slid into the Niagara River. That power plant supplied all of the electricity to New York City and beyond. We lived quite close to the power plant, and after a loud noise, the house shook mightily. This was an event. That night there was no power and thus no dinner at the prescribed time.

Once a week I was given cash for household expenses and I was expected to not ask for more. I had no access to the checkbook since it was assumed that I would not know how to manage money. A credit card was unheard of.

When I began my married life in Niagara Falls, I didn't know a soul except for his parents around the corner who were not the conversational or friendly type. I couldn't boil water let alone make a meal. I busied myself reading cookbooks, walking to the grocery store because I did not drive, and then come home to experiment. I discovered that I loved to cook. I was most at peace when I planted and worked in my small garden. Throughout my lifetime, working in a garden continued to be my therapy. I volunteered to be a Girl Scout leader at our nearby Catholic church which allowed me to make a few new friends, but most of all I wanted children to make me feel complete. I needed someone who would communicate with me and return my love.

# A WEE SEED OF DISCONTENT

I tried to get my handsome husband interested in romance. He just wasn't interested. One night after supper, I went upstairs, showered, perfumed and put on a sexy black lace peignoir, a part of my wedding trousseau. I came down the stairs in a grand entrance. His voice stopped me half way down. I was told sternly to go back upstairs and get some clothes on. Keep in mind that I was a beautiful 19-year old and starved for love and attention. I was crushed. He just didn't get it. After six months of marriage Jim asked me to hunt down a twin bed set at a house sale because he felt he was not getting enough rest for his job in a double bed. I did, according to his wishes. Many times, I asked myself if I was unattractive or was there something wrong with me? That handsome Jim was not inclined to love making. He felt that God meant sex for procreation not recreation, and that was that.

We used the rhythm method not to prevent conception but in fact, for the correct time for me to get pregnant. After two and a half years of going one way on what should have been a two-way street, our son Tim was born in 1956, followed by John in 1958, then quickly followed by Tom in 1959. Jim did not attend my labours, saying that I had a good doctor and his attendance was not necessary. Besides, he was needed at the mill. Tom was born at the end of April, a busy time for a milling/gardening business.

On May 22, 1959, when baby Tom was three weeks old, my father, at age 52, passed away unexpectedly because of a brain aneurysm. I arranged for a babysitter before Jim drove me over the International bridge to the Greyhound bus station in Niagara Falls, Ontario. There I boarded a bus to Toronto to make the funeral arrangements, sad and alone again. It was the 24th of May, a Canadian holiday, and through the three long days of the wake, my mother, brother and I sat alone. There were few visitors or flowers. Jim did come for the funeral Mass, after which we immediately drove home together in silence.

***

In our neighbourhood, a group of five neighbor couples began to meet on Saturday nights for dinner. One of the husbands, Mark, paid a lot of attention to me. He began calling me each morning to ask me how I was. Each call was full of general conversation, nothing intimate, but I was getting his vibes. Since I was not getting noticed at home, I loved his attention and wondered why my own husband could not give me a call once in a while during the day. Mark took his wife on a vacation to Bermuda and somehow managed to bring me back a gold libra charm and an azure blue knit cloche hat.

"To match my eyes," he said.

After a casual friendship of a few months we made a date to meet for lunch and an unspoken "something more" in Buffalo, a place that in those days seemed so very far away to me. We met and decided to behave, not to go further, and end what was hardly an affair. At least I got to go to Buffalo, twenty miles away. Our brief private friendship did plant a wee seed of discontent.

***

When Tim was a few weeks old, I decided that I would like to get a baby picture of him for posterity. I let my fingers do the walking in the yellow pages and found a company who would come to the house to snap a photo. It was called Peter Pan Studio. I made a call and set up an appointment. On the day of the sitting the doorbell rang and there, in front of me, looking very serious, stood the most handsome of men, tanned, and obviously Italian, wearing what looked like a designer suit. I invited him in. He awkwardly carried his camera over his shoulder. It was already attached to a tall tripod, draped with a black cloth. With few words he told me how to pose the baby, he snapped some pictures, told me he would mail the photos soon and left immediately. Something just didn't seem right. He just didn't look or act like a photographer. He looked more like an Italian Matinee Idol.

I loved the pictures. I called Peter Pan to set up an appointment to take a similar picture of John, born in 1958, followed by Tom, born in 1959. The pictures were all taken when each baby was eleven weeks old, and each time I let Peter in, I had that same funny feeling, but I was always happy with the pictures. Many years later I learned more about Peter. During World War II, he served with the 505th Parachute Infantry Regiment as a medic. He served in the Battle of the Bulge, and displayed great heroism, earning him the Purple Heart, 4 Bronze Stars, and many other medals. That would make him a war hero. Right. But wait, he also lived a life of crime. Later in life he was arrested by the FBI on charges of gambling and racketeering in association with the Buffalo Crime Family. I knew it. Peter Pan Studio was a front.

***

Blanche took no part in helping her daughter during those tiring days. Not once did my mother travel from Toronto to give me support, mentally or physically. Not even a phone call to express concern. Jim's mother seemed oblivious to the fact that I could use some help. Jim felt he should not help with children or household chores because, after all, he had to work all day. The same excuse was given for a midnight bottle or a crying infant. I was the one who got up. This was a time when cloth diapers were still in use, and three untrained babies made for lots of laundry. There were three cribs, and two high chairs. Although I was always tired, I found energy in the knowledge that those three handsome toe-heads were giving me the family unit that I had always yearned for. I would not be alone again. I loved being a mom in spite of the work. I did find a capable teenager who was able to babysit from time to time.

God, and the power of prayer to the good Saint Anne helped to bring us our first daughter. Judith Anne was born in June of 1961.

***

That same year Blanche decided to begin a new life in California. The thought of new opportunities in a warmer climate for both her and my brother Paul, excited her. She could also be with her long lost baby sister Helena.

In Toronto my brother Paul, who was then fifteen, was an outstanding hockey player and selected to go on to the Junior OHA. He had also been selected to continue school at Saint Michael's Choir School, a real honour. My mother didn't seem to consider the ramifications of what this move would do to Paul at this sensitive time in his life. She put an advertisement to rent our house in the Toronto Star. Three lawyers rented the fully furnished house on Gerrard Street. She applied for a green card, and off she went to the USA, dragging an unhappy Paul behind her.

Paul found it hard to adjust to California. He had lost his father, his Toronto friends, and the opportunity to play hockey. He finally found ice in the San Fernando Valley, which made life a bit happier for him.

My Aunt Helena knew someone, who knew someone, who got my mother a job as a cook at the prestigious Santa Monica Beach Club, a place where many of the 'stars' and their families gathered. My mother specialized in the creation of picture perfect delicious salads. Her job gave her the opportunity to order and use the best exotic food items flown in from faraway places, especially Hawaii.

***

Blanche was what one might call "light fingered". She could always rationalize why an owner or institution had too many, didn't need the item, or they deserved to lose the item. When Blanche made her annual trip to visit us in Niagara Falls, her grandchildren couldn't wait to see what Nana's extra big brown suitcase contained. Thanks to the Beach Club, once a year we had huge commercial sized cans of salted peanuts, the best tall cans of white albacore tuna, candy, new tea towels and various other goodies. "They'll never miss it", she would tell us. That story continues to make everyone in the family laugh.

At the age of fifty-five Blanche was a one-hundred twenty-pound beauty with charm that she could turn on with the twist of her little finger. The accentuated French speech pattern was the topper. She found an apartment in the Brentwood section of Los Angeles which was manageable because of the rent control regulations.

When she was lonesome in California, she would dress up like royalty, always wearing a dress she had recreated from the Goodwill store down a few blocks away on Barrington Avenue. Because she was there so often, they knew her by name. Her tip to me was to recreate something old by replacing the buttons with a few expensive new ones.

She would find her way to one of two upper class bars in Santa Monica, where she was able to meet many beaus, always professional men who enjoyed her company, dated her and took her to the best places.

Blanche always amazed me. In the mid 60's the actress June Lockhart was seen in the movie "Lassie" and on television in the series "Lost in Space". During that same time period of time Ms. Lockhart made a number of television commercials for Crest toothpaste. Ms. Lockhart knew my mother from the Beach Club, so she hired Blanche to take care of her mother on the set during the filming of films and many commercials. My mother loved the ambiance of the Lockhart residence where she picked up June's mother, then linger on the set. Another perk was the day long buffet of the best food stuff during the shoot. My mother told everyone, including our family, that she was Miss Lockhart's private secretary. I'll bet she brought an oversized and leak proof doggy bag each time she went! Leave it to Blanche to turn babysitting an infirmed lady into the words 'social secretary'.

***

While my very attractive mother was living the good life of Southern California, I was dealing with four children under five years old. One day I received a phone call from Blanche's former next door neighbour on Gerrard Street in Toronto. She told me that there was no doubt in her mind that the house had become a house of prostitution. I called the Toronto police, which was followed by a raid. The occupants were thrown off of the premises and arrested. I immediately put the house with all of the contents up for sale. Oh, how I wish I had some of that solid mahogany furniture now. I sold the house for $13,000. In Toronto's hot reality market, it is now valued at a million because of its downtown location.

***

In 1971, still beautiful at the age of sixty-three, she met and married a man younger then herself, who had that handsome German aristocratic look and one nasty personality. His name was Raymond Moesinger. He wore an ascot, was overbearing, was condescending and a loner.

My mother didn't seem unhappy. They lived in a rent-controlled apartment in the upscale neighbourhood of Brentwood, California. This proved to be a beneficial blessing because over a number of years, the rental market on her block skyrocketed. The Mezzaluna Café of O. J. Simpson fame was just around the corner and Nicole Brown lived two blocks away. After a time, her much loved baby sister Helena discovered that she had cancer and my mother was there to nurse her until the end. I faithfully kept in touch with her by phone. Her marriage and the nursing of her sister made her annual pilgrimages to see her grandchildren less frequent. Seeing her grandchildren was never a priority.

# A DREADFUL ACCIDENT

I was almost nine months pregnant with Tim when I took my driving test. I pushed the seat back as far as it would go and barely fit myself behind the wheel. A terrible wind and rain storm came through the city the night before. Trees were laying across many of the streets where I had to take the test. The examiner got into my car, and after a couple of blocks he told me to return to the starting point. He must have felt sorry for me because he passed me. Now that I had my driver's license, I had a bit more freedom. Joining and volunteering for the Saint Francis Guild of the local Catholic hospital offered an interesting diversion. Jim Allen's great Aunt had founded the group years before. Then it was called the Saint Mary's Sewing Circle. I served on their Board of Directors and chaired the first St Francis Guild Ball. I also became a member of the Deveaux Mothers Club, an eclectic group who met once a month to discuss topical issues of the day. I could now chat and share with my interesting friends.

Although my young family took up most of my time, I felt that working in the community would make my life more exciting and well-rounded. I took on a Girl Scout troop with meetings in my house or in the backyard. For three summers I volunteered at Camp Windy Meadows, the local Girl Scout summer camp, which was an opportunity to use the skills learned at Lake

Couchiching in Canada. When the three boys were young, I became a den mother for the Cub Scouts.

***

In 1963, nine founding members, including myself, developed and began a Montessori School in Niagara Falls, one of the first in Western New York. A certified Montessori teacher had to be hired, and special equipment had to be bought in Holland. A location, a closed Catholic elementary school, was converted to suit the special needs of a Montessori classroom. The basic principle of the Montessori method permits the very young child to execute free expression revealing his or her needs and aptitudes. We began with 60 students. Today, after 54 years, the school remains successful and is now located at Stella Niagara Park in Lewiston, New York.

By 1964 the space in our house on Dorchester Road was too small, and my tummy was stretched out again because I was carrying number five. It seemed like the right time to move to a bigger house.

***

There was a summer heat wave on that August day when we moved a few blocks away to 926 Vanderbilt Avenue. Daughter Joan was due a month away in September. Piles of storage boxes and furniture had been delivered in the Allen Milling Company's truck on Sunday and on Monday, Jim went to work. I was left alone in the oppressive heat to empty cartons and organize our new house. Well, not really alone, because my four rambunctious children, under the age of eight, were discovering every inch of their new house. That morning I had dressed the four minimally, without shirts and in short pants and sneakers because it was so hot out. The air was still and without even a breeze. There was no air-conditioning so all of the windows were up as far as they could go. The two entrances were located on either side of the house, and across the front, on the street side, was a long raised grey porch which could only be accessed by inside doors off of the living room.

By mid-morning son Tim went outside and found a hose. He pointed the water through the open living room window, soaking the back of the television which had been placed under the window, which then blew up because the set was turned on. The smoke was still rising from the back of the television when I heard five-year-old Tommy screaming outside. I found the closest door facing the street and found myself on the front porch which had no exit.

A neighbourhood dog had already bitten skinny little Tommy on the naked back and now had his buttocks in his jaw, shaking him like a rag doll. I climbed over the porch rail, cleared the prickly Barberry bushes and landed with a great thud. The dog was so frightened that he let go. The new across-the-street neighbor was also frightened. She ran over because she was concerned not for Tommy but for me in my very large eighth month condition. She introduced herself as Rose Moscati and offered to watch the remaining three children while I took Tom to the hospital for a tetanus shot. Welcome to the neighbourhood! In spite of the porch acrobatics, a healthy Joan Louise was born a month later in September.

***

The everyday rhythm of keeping a house and a growing family organized made the days fly by. Part of the demands of motherhood included my many trips to the grocery store. We lived in the Deveaux area of Niagara Falls. In June of 1972, I drove to the grocery store, going down Lewiston Road past the 44 acres of Deveaux School. Something about the campus seemed different as I drove by. I slowed down to take a better look. It looked to me as though a number of red flags were forming a new street down the middle of the grass next to the main entrance of the school. While shopping, I kept thinking about those flags. It was no secret that the elite private boys' school, operating since the mid-1850s, had financial problems. I decided to take a much closer look on the way home. My second look convinced me that something was happening.

As soon as I returned home, I called my friend and neighbor Mayor O'Laughlin and asked him what was going on. He seemed to be in the dark regarding this matter. The beautiful brick English Tudor homes of the city professionals were situated around the perimeters of Deveaux School. Those were the people that I called upon to come together and investigate. The Deveaux citizens group was formed, a group that included a city councilman, a city planner, two attorneys, a physician's wife who offered to host the first meeting, and myself.

Our investigation revealed that a 200-unit low income housing unit was being planned on 10 acres of school grounds under the aegis of the Urban Development Corporation (UDC). This New York State organization had the ability to supersede local zoning.

A partnership between a local architect, a local construction company and the Deveaux School Board of Trustees had moved forward in silence. When the plan came to light, the surrounding neighbours were furious because of the lack of transparency. They envisioned the real possibility of their property values plummeting. A low-income housing unit already existed four blocks away that, at the time, only had 30% occupancy and which was falling apart. Deveaux residents were ready to fight the proposal. Over the next few months I attended a number of meetings. Excellent reporting by the local Gazette published enlightening newspaper articles. UDC finally relented because of the furor. We won!

***

New York State Office of Parks and Recreation acquired the property in 2001. Today, as a park, there are baseball diamonds, a playground, an ice skating rink, a nature trail, seasonal restrooms, and biking. A small area of old forest growth is present inside the park. Every time I drive by the Deveaux Woods State Park, I am very happy that I took the time to investigate and rally the troops or this park would not exist.

***

Mary Helen Allen was born in January of 1969. I remained in the hospital after she was born and the doctor performed a hysterectomy. For me there would be no more procreation, and so, as inadequate as it had been before, no more physical relationship with my husband. How sad.

***

Jim referred to, and always called me, mom. I wanted to be called "honey", "babe", or something else equally endearing. I wanted to scream, "I am not your mother!"

***

His mother, was Clara O'Brien, born in Niagara Falls, NY in 1901. Her mother, Mary Bampfield, was from Niagara Falls, Ontario, born into a family with history and old money. Clara lived as a true Edwardian English woman, quiet and reserved, never showing any emotion. Her life was determined by her husband's wishes and the clock. Every morning, even on the hottest of summer days, she donned her nylons, slip, dress and mid-heel shoes. Her pocket watch always hung around her neck on a thin black cord. I'm sure that she never ever wore a bathing suit, shorts or even slacks.

Her life as Clara Allen was lived by the time. Cocktails were served at 5:00 p.m. sharp, and always served in cut crystal glasses accompanied by crisp linen cocktail napkins. At 6 p.m. sharp, she served dinner at a table set with English bone china, sterling, crystal and more linen napkins. The only thing missing was a downstairs staff. She seemed cold to me and I was a little afraid of her, but I should not have been. She suffered from mental issues that were a dark family secret. Was it her mother, father or her overbearing and controlling husband that aggravated this sickness? Could it have been caused by the death of her newborn son also called James? Who knows? She was on medications that should not have been mixed with alcohol. On Sunday, September

27, 1970, she was entertaining guests when she lost her balance, tripping over a side table. The thin crystal cocktail glass that she was holding shattered onto the stone hearth. She continued to fall, landing on a sharp shard of the glass. She severed her carotid artery and was bleeding to death. In shock, Jim's father telephoned us because we lived around the corner.

We rushed over. I sat on the floor and cradled her head in my lap. She was covered in blood. Someone handed me a towel which I placed into the hole in her neck, but she was already gone. There was blood everywhere, but a lot had seeped into the thin space between the hardwood and the stone hearth. The next day Jim took two of the girls and went into the basement to clean up the pool of red blood on the floor.

Judy aged nine asked him what that "stuff" was.

His answer was "It's rusty water coming out of the furnace". That must have been a difficult task for him. Judy still remembers that scene.

***

Four of our children were enrolled at the local parochial school. I took an active part as an officer of the St. Teresa's Mother's Club since they were always raising money to keep the school alive. The club mothers never seemed to warm up to the new parish priest because he was what now would be called "a nerd". I, on the other hand, thought he was wonderful, and he became my good friend. We were kindred spirits because we both were interested in the power of the arts. He was a quiet, bespectacled intellectual, with a penchant for Medieval Illuminated Manuscripts. He was no-nonsense and didn't respond to a sports conversation, a must in Niagara Falls. He did however respond to any conversation having to do with the arts. I never discussed the direction of my marriage or my home life with him.

***

One day I received a phone call from Father O'Heron. It seems that there was a woman that he knew who lived in Bradford, Pennsylvania, and who had a number of Illuminated Manuscripts and other fine art pieces that she was going to either sell or bequeath. She had acquired them from her late millionaire husband T. Edward Hanley. She was hosting an open house/viewing of some of her husband's collection and he wondered if I would be interested in going with him to keep him company. He knew I would appreciate the art work. It sounded like an adventure to me. I said that I would go.

***

Tullah Hanley deserves a note of introduction. She was born in Hungary. Her mother was Egyptian, born in a harem and adopted by Hungarian parents. I couldn't make this up. At age fifteen she came to America where she performed her own classical style of Egyptian and African dance in music and vaudeville halls. When she was twenty-four she met and married T. Edward Hanley, a millionaire oil baron and art collector from Bradford, PA. who was much older than her. They shared a passion for art and until his death in 1968, she took an active role in his collection. She continued their philanthropy to major museums and universities.

In Bradford she was called "Bradford's Merry Widow", especially after she published her book called 'The Art of Love and the Love of Art." She was now widowed.

Local tongues wagged when she set up workshops on the second floor of her enormous building. The classes were designed to teach young boys small appliance repair which would keep young boys occupied and keep them off of Bradford's streets. She was the subject of a local police investigation.

When the children were young, even going to Buffalo was significant, so the drive to Bradford seemed to never end. We drove through the Allegheny State Park, past many deer whose eyes flashed yellow as we rode by in the dark, then across the state border into Pennsylvania. After a mile we were in Bradford, PA. We pulled up and parked in front of what seemed to be a large two story furniture store located at 24 Main Street.

I gasped as I went through the front entrance. The huge space was dimly lit. Art work was hanging from ceiling to floor, frame to frame, two stories high. Important and signed canvases by major artists, canvases that took your breath away, were hung next to Kmart pot boilers.

There were very few women in attendance, just dozens and dozens of priests from nearby St. Bonaventure University and beyond, all hoping that their institution would benefit from Mrs. Hanley's largesse. There were many bars set up across the floor space but there was no food. Father O'Heron wandered one way and I went in another direction checking out this unusual scene.

There was one main staircase and underneath that staircase a section had been curtained off. It was a makeshift dressing room for Tullah, the hostess. I grabbed a glass of wine and watched in awe. Every half hour Tullah would emerge from behind the curtain, dressed in a different colorful and very gauzy kaftan that set off her leggy youthful figure. She was a startling vision from head to toe. Her head was wrapped in a turban which matched her outfit, which was then set off by her Nefertiti eyes and six-inch heels, finishing her harem look.

The food finally appeared. Four slim and beautiful young boys carried in buckets and buckets of Kentucky Fried Chicken and set them out near the bars, or on a chair, minus plates or napkins. I guess the word casual would really apply.

I wandered upstairs. Large rooms had been made into obvious workspaces. In one corner was Tullah's bedroom, complete with an altar and burning incenses. That evening, and Tullah, would forever be etched in my mind.

# MAISON BLANCHE CATERING

In spite of my beautiful children, I was becoming more and more unhappy. I decided to attend the annual St. Francis Guild fashion show at the last minute. Sitting there I found myself overwhelmed with an urgent need to run away. The venue was the Hotel Niagara, just two blocks from Canada. I left before the show was over and headed for the Rainbow Bridge. I didn't have a plan, I just had to get away and be by myself. I used my credit card at the Duty Free shop to buy a bottle of Canadian Club. I was going to head for Toronto but why, since there was nothing left there for me. Immediately in front of me at the other end of the bridge was the Brock Hotel. I parked, entered and asked for the best room in the house. The gentleman at the desk said the Honeymoon Suite, with a direct view of Niagara Falls, was available. I didn't ask what it cost, I just said that I would take it. I had no suitcase, just my purse and that bottle of booze.

The room was truly romantic, which made me even sadder. It had a large picture window facing the falls themselves. I was alone, so I poured myself a stiff drink, followed by another. I laid on the bed crying and fell into a sound sleep. I woke up in the middle of the night starving, but poured down another tumbler of CC.

Morning came and now I had to assess what I had done. What were my children thinking? What was I going to say to them? I walked into the bathroom and dumped the rest of the bottle into the toilet. I slept some more. I came to the conclusion that my spirit was broken because I was totally exhausted trying to be a perfect mother, wife, housekeeper, cook, auxiliary breadwinner and citizen.

I anxiously drove home to face the music. Everything seemed so normal when I walked into the house that I was almost disappointed. Jim had told the children that I was on a business trip and so no one had missed me. Jim did not confront me for an explanation. My life didn't change. I just continued to soldier on.

I tried going over to visit our parish church on several occasions, thinking I could pray in the shadow of the altar for strength. Sadly, the doors were always locked.

I was unhappy on a number of fronts, one of which was the meager and stagnant amount of household money given to me every Friday night. Kmart, followed by many more big box stores, had moved into our city, and Allen Milling Company was beginning to feel ever increasing competition. Jim's business could not match the prices for grass seed, salt, lawn mowers, dog food and more, now available elsewhere. There would be no pay increase for our growing family in the foreseeable future. I needed to find a way to produce income while staying at home and not neglecting my children.

***

During the 60's having a cocktail party in your home or having a lady's tea was the social norm for many hosts. In a conversation, my friend Grace, who hated to cook, told me she was going to have a cocktail party for her real estate friends. Would I help her, and she would pay me? That 1966 party began my chapter in life as a caterer. I loved to cook with fuss and imagination, and this was a job that I could do without leaving the house. I never advertised but word of mouth brought me more business than I needed. People who had my telephone number would call and ask for X number of hors d'oeuvres, cookies or tarts, and then come to my side door to pick them up. The children soon learned how to put together cardboard packing boxes, and how to cut onions, celery, radishes or bread on their lunch hour from their school which was located just around the corner. The strict rule was that everything was counted and sneaking a piece of anything was never allowed. In return they benefited by enjoying shrimp, crab, pate and chicken livers at a very early age. Today each of six children is an adventurous eater and a marvelous and creative cook.

As the children grew, so did my business. I cooked for Boy Scout dinners, wakes and weddings, holiday and home parties and I cooked entire meals, including dessert, for a number of business professionals whose wives passed the meal off as their own to their guests. My lips are sealed since, sadly, usually their wives were alcoholics.

Cooking is a patient and creative art form and many times I had to have both. A local politician hired me to cater his daughter's wedding at the Officers Club at Old Fort Niagara in the Village of Youngstown N.Y. This historic venue had not been used in many years. His wife and I had agreed on the number of people who would attend, and I planned the amount of finger foods accordingly. The event had barely started when one of my servers came to me and said that the food on the trays was almost all gone. How could that be? It seems that the father was running for re-election in the village and everyone he had met in the previous month he had verbally invited to his daughter's wedding. They must have all come on his oral invitation. I immediately jumped into my car, drove six miles to Helm's Grocery store in the next village of Lewiston, and bought anything and everything that could be used as a bite to eat. I got back to the wedding and started creating. The results were amazing, and the bride and her family didn't even realize that there had been a problem.

I had many adventures in the business which was called "Maison Blanche" after my mother. I always arrived at each job with a big pile of white tea towels and a roll of butcher paper. It was amazing to me to see how dirty people kept their kitchens. Local socialites who put on such a show were always the worst.

I did a home wedding for one such woman whose hippie daughter was pregnant. They lived in an outstanding 1830 historic home, complete with a white picket fence. It was to be an outdoor, black tie affair. There were flowers and ribbons everywhere. Indoors, behind a closed door, their kitchen was disgusting. It poured rain and the guests were forced into a very small inside space. The bride came down the wide staircase outfitted in a straight white satin gown which was slightly bulged through her middle section. She held a single drooped Calla Lily wrapped in a wide white satin bow. Her hair was bedraggled, and she looked like she herself would wilt with the humidity and the number of guests jammed into the house. The groom, with his long stringy hair, stood at the bottom of the winding grand staircase, uncomfortably dressed in a tux, beads, and sandals. The parents of the bride were distraught because the pouring rain had spoiled their plans.

Immediately after the ceremony, the bride, groom and their friends retired to the garage attic to drink beer, while I tried to squeeze through the remaining guests to serve dinner. The bride's mother wept and wept, and I wondered why I was putting myself through all of this. It was so hot, and it was so much work!

Not too long after the Lewiston wedding I was asked to cater a wedding at the Knights of Columbus hall across the Niagara River, in Niagara Falls, Ontario. Over a number of days I shopped, prepared food, and then on the appointed day, already tired, I loaded our old woodie station wagon. I picked up my two servers and headed for the International bridge. After many questions at the bridge, we went to the wedding reception site. Everything went well, until the wedding cake portion of the evening. One of the servers came into the kitchen to say that a guest had spilled hot coffee on her lap. I grabbed a pile of tea towels and ran to where a very large lady was sitting. She lifted her dress to above her knees and pointed to her stockings. I wiped her knees, but she kept pointing, now at her calf. I bent lower. Now she pointed to her ankle, so I knelt down on the floor in front of her and wiped her ankle. At that very moment I had an epiphany. Why was I on my hands and knees in front of this rude superior woman. I got up, packed my things and returned home exhausted. That was the proverbial straw that broke the camel's back. I would never cater again.

***

Over the course of the next week I gave a lot of thought to what I could do that would allow me to work but be home for the children when it was necessary. I came up with the idea of wallpapering. I bought two ladders, cutting boards, buckets, sponges and brushes, and spread the word among my friends that I was available.

The wife of a senior corporate executive of one of the local industrial plants called me one day to ask me if I would cater another cocktail party in their grand and impressive home on the heights of the Niagara escarpment. Previously I had catered a number of parties for her and the food was always a great success. I told her that I was no longer catering, and that I was now in the wallpaper business. She asked what I would charge to do her husband's den in a hunter green plaid paper. I gave her price and hung the paper. She was very pleased with the results. Not long after, she called again. She had purchased paper for her living and dining room. It was white on white. I explained to both her and her husband that no matter how careful I was, and I was very exact, the seams would show in some places. I also told her that no matter where I was into the job, I had to leave by four in the afternoon to be home for my children. They said they understood, and we came to a financial agreement.

I started on the following Monday. I setup my new equipment in the wide hall, then began to take off all of the wall plug plates. As I went into the living room, it was hard not notice Mr. K. sitting in an armchair watching me. He stared at me each time I bent to remove the remaining plates. I felt very uncomfortable. When I got up on my tall ladder and struggled to remove the Kirsch triple rod curtain fixtures, he just sat there in silence, not offering to help as I stretched from side to side. He just leered. I felt that he was visually undressing me.

That week I continued to work until I was almost finished. Only three strips to go. I reminded Mrs. K. that as per our agreement I would leave at four and return the next morning to finish and clean up.

That evening while my family was eating their dinner the phone rang. It was Mrs. K. She said not to come back tomorrow because her husband was very displeased with the job, and furthermore, he would not pay me. I was really angry, but I chalked it up to a learning lesson, and besides, I found Mr. K. uncomfortable and lecherous. I did not want to deal with him again, but life had another meeting in my future.

Ten years later, a couple of old friends invited me to spend a week in Hilton Head, South Carolina. They had rented a beautiful space, surrounded by other properties owned by former fellow executives of the company he had retired from. They were excited to tell us that we were invited to an evening cocktail party. The glamorous setting was straight out of the movies. There were many chic glamorous people meeting outdoors for food, wine and music. At one point I felt a pair of riveted eyes boring into me.

A gentleman came over to me and said, “don’t I know you from somewhere?”

I answered “no” and he continued to question me.

The man was Mr. K. who, years before didn’t pay me for a wall papering job well done. I just walked away.

# SAM

I moved to the area in the 50's which was a time of prosperity in Niagara Falls because of the building of the new Niagara Power Plant. It was in the 60's and 70's that I really learned about everything "Niagara Falls". The majority of people that lived there had no desire to explore beyond the city, not even to go to Youngstown or Buffalo, both a short distance away. They enjoyed sports, beer, mystery novels, bingo, tractor pulls and all things Italian, especially the food. Very few were interested, or seem to value the arts or early education.

***

I always felt that a parent should treat each child in the family as a single individual. It was obvious that each of my children had special skills that needed to be nurtured. All six children were artistic, and they all expressed it in a different way. When Tim, the oldest, was ready for high school, we sent him to Bishop Duffy, the Catholic high school. I asked if they had an art program and they said no. Because it was Catholic, and his father had attended that school, we sent him anyway. My children were never interested in sports. During his first year there, his teachers pushed him into joining the track team.

The next year we sent him to Trott Vocational School to study drafting, the closest thing to an art program that I could find.

Bishop Duffy was typical of all of the other high schools in the area. They viewed the arts as less important in the educational scheme of things, including their budgeting. Sports were always deemed important and always included in the budget.

Tim and Tom played the piano and organ, John exhibited a leaning to be an artisan, his great hands working with wood and clay. Tom was interested in theatre. Judy was interested in dance and theatre. Joan showed amazing creativity in her love of cooking. I knew by the time Mary Helen was four that she was destined to be an artist. I often wondered how my children would be able to enhance their individual gifts of creativity in the Niagara Falls educational environment. I thought what the community needed, and deserved, was a facility that would cater to artistically bent children like my own.

***

In the early '70s, I gathered a small committee of people interested in promoting artists and art groups in the area. This group of people included a representative from the Little Theatre, the Niagara Society of Artists, the Niagara Falls Philharmonic, the Niagara Civic Ballet, Niagara University Theatre, the local library, the Leaders Forum Singers, and the Music School of Niagara. Among this organizing group were a few individuals who ascribed to the importance of the arts in a community. One of those people was a man who I will call Sam. I represented the Niagara Civic Ballet because my daughter Judy was training with them.

We all met several times during the next two years, always keeping in mind that there should be a facility in Niagara Falls that would include all of the art groups under one roof. We legally incorporated as a non-profit agency and formed the Niagara Council of the Arts. Members of the group hired me as the first Executive Director. There was no salary, no budget, only a vision. Someone told me that we could apply to the New York State Council on the Arts (NYSCA) for start-up funding. I wrote my first grant to NYSCA at my kitchen table supported by Sharon Onevelo who was with the Theater department of Niagara University. My six children, including Mary Helen, then four years old, ran in and out of the kitchen and throughout the house. We were not deterred. Although I had never written a grant before, we got the paperwork written and into the mail by the deadline. We were successful in our request, and now we finally had a small budget to work with.

One day I received a phone call from Sam, who was interested in politics and always knew what was going on at city hall. The word was out that when the new library, designed by the famous architect Paul Rudolph, would be completed by 1974, the old Carnegie Library would be vacant, and could be made into the perfect Art Center. Sam thought that we should explore the possibility together.

I agreed to go with him to City Hall for a visit to our colorful and newsworthy Mayor E. Dent Lackey. I had written a long list of reasons why the city needed this kind of facility. I named the many interested organizations that could use the space. I gave examples of who could possibly fund the project. To our amazement, the mayor stood up from his desk, pushed his chair back, and pronounced that the Carnegie building was ours to use, plus $17,000 in start-up money. Since the building belonged to the city, he added total maintenance. During the next month the offer was ratified by the city council. With that pronouncement, my life would be changed dramatically and forever.

The Arts Council now had a two-story high space, plus a basement, in which we could have art exhibitions, concerts, have poetry readings or have small dance recital. Sam and I made an appointment to visit the internationally acclaimed sculptor Mary Metcalfe Lang who lived in Niagara Falls. We told her our plans for the building but explained to her that we really needed $1,000 to refinish the wooden floor in the rotunda. Sam used all of his charm while stroking her beloved long-haired black cat Midnight nestled in his lap. He hated and was allergic to cats. That day we left her house with the check and excitement in the fact that our project was moving forward.

The historic and artistic merits of the buildings spoke for themselves. I had the building placed on the State Registry of Historic Buildings, followed by inclusion on the National Historic Registry.

Just after the rotunda floor was refinished into gleaming hardwood, a stooped older woman with a strong foreign accent came up the marble stairs to see me. Her name was Rose Mossell. She said that before World War II she was a concert pianist, playing in concert halls all across Europe. She had escaped to America with her only important possession, her prized Bechstein Concert Grand piano. She had it in storage and wanted to bring it to the rotunda space, so she could play it every day. We decided to bring the piano into the building. Every day she came to play her beloved instrument. During the winter months she would bring in blankets to keep her piano warm. She was loaded with arthritis, her fingers crooked and knobby, but that didn't stop her from playing. The piano was the perfect artistic touch and sound for the rotunda.

The Niagara Council of the Arts' newly acquired building was built in 1903. In typical Carnegie style there were nine wide marble stairs centered from the beautiful glass and wooden entrance doors. At the top of the stairs, on either side, were two 11th century urns acquired from a church in Flanders and donated by the artist, writer and traveler Mary Metcalfe Lange. Just past the top landing were two wide walnut swinging doors each with brass door plates with an egg and dart design. Two large reading rooms were situated inside the doors on the left and on the right. Both rooms had high, pristine stained-glass insets on the ceiling. These two rooms would make an ideal gallery space. There was a two-story rotunda beyond the two galleries. The second story had a thick opaque glass floor with a half circle of brass and a decorative wrought iron railing. Sam said that he found a construction company who would remove the glass floor for the scrap. Interestingly, a few years later, pieces of that beautiful wrought iron appeared in each of the windows of Sam's home for security.

Sam was hard not to notice. At board meetings he stood out from all of those present. China blue eyes were set into a perpetually tanned face, perfect teeth, a melt your heart smile all topped off by prematurely snow-white, stylishly cut hair. He always appeared totally absorbed in each proposed project. He was utterly charming, attentive, interesting, witty, and flirtatious to male and female alike. I had heard that although he didn't wear a wedding ring, he was married and that he was a womanizer.

Over the next two years Sam and I had many business meetings together with member art groups who wanted space in the new Art Center. We put together a building committee who planned the implementation of their space needs. The arts council became the newest member of the New York State Alliance of Arts Councils, a statewide art advocacy group. Meetings were held on a regular basis around the state. One such morning meeting was planned for Batavia, New York, which was within driving distance from home. Sam suggested that we should both attend. On the way home, we had lunch together in a romantic country inn, had a glass of wine and although my motives that day began as pure, the rest of the afternoon became a part of my personal history. I never ever thought that he could be interested in me, the mother of six. I came completely under his spell.

The next day I drove to Kmart to buy the years #1 record bestseller, Roberta Flack's "The First Time Ever I Saw Your Face". Surely it was written just for me. I played it and played it at every opportunity. My daughter Mary Helen, five years old, told me to stop playing that stupid song.

Sam had a strategy which he used time and time again in the following years. He only chose vulnerable women for his victims. He knew how to solidify a relationship. Every morning I would pick up the arts council mail at the main post office. There was always a single page love letter waiting for me, written in his small tight hand. There were many phone calls during the day, inquiring about how my day was going. In our conversations it was always "WE" can do this, or "WE" can do that. He made me feel special and he made me feel loved. He had me completely engaged and I was hooked. We moved into the Carnegie Library in early 1974. I think subconsciously that I felt that we were moving into our own personal space. Funny how your possessed mind can fool you.

***

Later that year, the house next door to Sam's house was for sale and he encouraged me to buy it. He said that WE could fix and decorate it together. It was a truly beautiful 13 room house very close to the Niagara river. Jim Allen went along with the move without a peep, question or hesitation. Surely, he had to know what was going on in plain sight. I yearned for him to confront me, but nothing.

That same year, 1974, my children were growing up. Tim was 18 and finishing high school. John was 16, Tom 15, followed by Judy 13, Joan 10 and Mary Helen 5 years old. As much as my boys disliked Sam, they liked the new house because there was a lot of room in the back of the yard to pursue their passion of rebuilding and fixing old cars, and it was a shorter walk to the Niagara gorge where they spent many hours in all of the four seasons. The gorge remains a place that they love. Judy and Mary Helen's friends all lived nearby so they were happy. Joan became Sam's wife's devoted pseudo daughter. His wife was a marvelous baker who taught and reinforced Joan's love of cooking. She was always next door trying some new recipe with his lonesome wife and her constant companion, a little dog named

Missy. One summer she suggested that the three girls and I should spend a week at the cottage that she and Sam had rented on Lake Erie. Sam and I carpooled back and forth to work in Niagara Falls, while she and Missy stayed with my daughters during the day.

That year Mary Helen began school at the nearby public school. I believe the boys at least suspected something was going on, but of course, I never brought up the subject.

***

With time, the true Sam began to reveal himself and I learned the true meaning of the word womanizer. After a couple of years in the Art Center, the daily letters stopped, and the phone calls were less frequent. On many days we had breakfast or lunch together. His interest in me had waned but had not entirely stopped. I noticed that at board meetings he would not hang back to be with me but left with an attractive blonde board member who had a son who she couldn't manage. She was also having marital problems. Sam to her rescue. He had a motorcycle and on many Saturday afternoons I rode behind him to some interesting destination. She bought her own motorcycle so that they could ride away together towards the sunset. I was so jealous, and I was heartbroken. I am embarrassed to say that one night after a meeting I actually drove through downtown parking lots trying to follow them until they got away. More tears. Over the next ten years a steady parade of vulnerable, sweet women came under his spell. Some were one-night stands, some relationships lasted for months, and one lasted for years.

During those years I was constantly waiting for even a crumb of his time and attention. One day he called me to go with him at lunchtime because he had an electrical job to do. I went with him because I just wanted to be with him. We drove at high noon to the old closed and abandoned jail on Main Street and parked in front of the building. Lots of traffic was passing by in both directions.

He said, “wait here”.

He took out a large canvas tool bag from the back of his car, sashayed up to the front of the building when the sun was at high noon, and removed two beautiful antique glass light fixtures from the sides of the jail’s front entrance doors. Traffic continued to drive by as he casually carried them back to the car and place them in the trunk. They ended up on his patio doors in the back of his house.

When the new Art Center needed shrubs to landscape the front of the building, I sat in the car as he removed bushes by putting a chain around the greenery of an abandoned car dealership. It was so exciting and a secret between us. It was so wrong, and I regret this so much since I never was dishonest before or after these events.

In the new house, my upstairs bedroom window looked down onto his driveway next door, and I watched his nightly coming and goings in self-abuse. His next victim was a young widowed woman, with two young children. She was the owner of a very successful travel agency and Sam would be there to help her with her business. Oh, sure! That was followed by a year-long relationship with his new eighteen-year old secretary. He was teaching her his business methods. He bragged to me with a smile that her family would often invite him to dinner because he was so kind to their daughter. Did they know that he had recently built a small apartment in the back of his office building to teach her, shall we say, housekeeping? Early on I wondered why he always carried a gun, always hidden on the side of his calf or in a holster strapped under his arm. I now knew why. I guess that was one of the things that made him exciting to me. When I was with him, I told myself that I was the only one in his universe, even though I knew that I was only fooling myself. He took an active role in the new art center and the arts council, so he was always somewhere in the picture for the next twelve years.

# THE NIAGARA COUNCIL ON THE ARTS

When I began as Executive Director, there was no guide or template regarding the direction the organization should take. During the following eleven years in the Carnegie building, the space was used seven days a week including many evenings. There were music lessons, children's art classes called ArtWheels, ballet demonstrations, concerts, art exhibitions, poetry readings, rock, coin, flower and bird shows. Some of these events required a small tuition or rental fee, which then increased our budget in order to help pay the staff. We also had a membership program which allowed a member certain discounts and a monthly newsletter that offered a calendar of events for all of the Niagara County art happenings.

Our Board of Directors were individuals who could help accomplish our important community mission. They were residents from every corner of the county, not just from Niagara Falls and I made sure that the board makeup was inclusive before it was ever required. I found a perfect and generous attorney, a fiscal person who was the COO of our local hospital, an artist, Father O'Heron, my intellectual religious friend, someone from tourism, and men and women with senior positions with local banks and the industrial plants headquartered in the city. Their services were always free and appreciated. They could leverage dollars for our budget and permit entrée into many sectors of our population.

In these beginning years, we started with a staff made up of a secretary, two full time art teachers and myself. Over the next thirty years our staff grew. We added an Assistant Director who took care of the day to day finances and our NYS regrant program (Decentralization). I was aware that accountability to all of our funding sources, Federal, State, County and City was a must. A public relations person and dozens of sub-contracted artists and musicians for public and school events also needed to be paid.

The New York State Council of the Arts staff was so impressed with our Board that for many years I traveled all around the State as a consultant to arts organizations, large and small, who needed help in board management. The nice thing about serving as a consultant was that you could say what the group didn't want to hear, then leave with a sigh and an amen.

We started with an annual budget of $19,000 and when I retired in 2000 our annual budget was $550,000, with thousands of dollars more in in-kind services. Each program required me to discover and write the initial grant, many times followed by a midway report and final paperwork. As the population declined over the years in Niagara County, so did the local economy. Most of the corporations moved out of town. Fundraising became more difficult and fund raising became a big part of my job.

After our initial start-up grant from the New York State Council of the Arts (NYSCA), I pursued financial help from any NYSCA division that was applicable to our art center. I developed programs and funding through Facilities, Arts Education, Literature, Music, Folk Arts, Presenting, and Decentralization, which was a regrant program.

I became known to the staff of NYSCA, and they responded by asking me to become a Panelist. In that capacity, I was required to attend their meetings in New York City, sometimes twice a month. Panelists received copies of the grant applications submitted to the State and reviewed them before attending New York City meetings where decisions would be made.

During that same time period, I learned about an organization located in Huntington, New York, called the Alliance of New York State Arts Organizations. Its mission was to advocate for continued and increased financial support for the arts (NYSCA) in the New York State budget. It represented large and small organizations throughout the State who would travel to Albany, New York, before the budget process. I was humbled by their offer for me to serve on their Board of Directors and I accepted. I realized the importance of their mission because NYSCA had given the Niagara Council of the Arts so much financial support. I was now a panel member of NYSCA and I was aware of how hard their staff worked with the money in their tight budget.

I felt that advocating for increased funding for the arts at all government levels was an important part of my job. I invited all of the Niagara County arts/tourism groups to form an organization called the Cultural Alliance of Niagara County (CAN). After many years, this group is still active and well.

***

Every now and again on one of my dealings with either of these State organizations, someone would ask me what college I had attended. I felt strangely incomplete without a college degree. At the time, New York State was beginning a new college program called Empire State College. The school gave me credit for some of my Canadian Grade XIII. With a thirteen-room house and seven people to tend to, plus a very busy job, I cross-registered at Niagara University and Niagara Community College. In 1977, after two years, I earned a Bachelor of Science degree in Arts Administration. I felt fulfilled even though Jim Allen did not attend my graduation ceremony. Sam supported me and did attend. I felt very proud of myself.

***

I flushed out dollars from the NYS Division for Youth and NYS Criminal Justice. That was an easy task since the depressing numbers, taken straight from the Niagara County census, were there for the picking. Locally the Niagara County Legislature, the City of Niagara Falls, and the local Division for Youth gave wonderful support. I also received funds from State-wide, non-profit cultural groups such as the NYS Meet the Composer program, Affiliate Artists, NYS Poets and Writers, Inc., and Poets in the Schools. I was always careful to keep separate accounts for each program.

***

I had to keep politicians at the State, County, and local government happy. The politics of the job always weighed like a stone around my neck. I worked under four mayors. Many times,

I had to grit my teeth and zip my mouth. One of these mayors had a vision contrary to what the general public wanted or could understand, but at least he had imagination. Two mayors were pleasant but not at all bright, and one was an absolute toad, with a Napoleonic ego and a small stature to match. A gold malocchio was displayed on his hairy chest underneath an unbuttoned open shirt. I just had to smile, keep programming, and show positive results. When a member of the Niagara Falls City Council and a former Board member was charged with bribery, he served his Community Service working in my office.

One evening I received a phone call at home from our local County legislator. He served as the Chairman of the County Finance Committee, and in true Niagara Falls fashion, his sister served as the Chairman of the County Youth Bureau. He had read my advertisement in our local paper for the position of a certified art teacher. It seems that his nephew needed a job. I explained that we had many applications and that the person that we hired had to be qualified. He reminded me that I received funding from both the County and the County Division for Youth, and he strongly suggested that it would be wise for me hire his nephew. I told him that we would take a very close look at his application. We did not hire his nephew. The next week I received another call at home.

"Listen you c---, I'll make sure that you'll never receive another cent from Niagara County", said the Legislator.

I gasped in shock and hung up the phone. The paperwork that I sent him annually had a list of the prestigious members of our

Board of Directors. We continued to get funding for the following years.

I found interesting ways to earn income by having unique fundraisers. No one had ever approached the New York Power Authority to use their beautiful new building located next to the water in Lewiston for an event. Built of glass and situated next to and over the Niagara River and gorge, it was the perfect setting for a catered black-tie dinner. An affirmative answer made that fundraiser a success and was a great vehicle for positive PR for the Power Authority.

The "Waste Water Wiggle" took place in the newly built Waste Water Treatment Plant, with little plastic bags of sludge as favors. The money raised was often used as a match for other funding sources.

***

I began a travel program called Road Scholar in 1979. That June I advertised a trip to Toronto to see the "King Tut" exhibition at the Art Gallery of Ontario. The package included a box lunch, entrance tickets and dinner in a Toronto restaurant. I sold enough tickets to fill three buses on three successive Saturdays.

In order to participate, the participant had to be a member of the Arts Council, which increased our membership revenues over the next thirty-five years. It was a new source of income for ever expanding list of new programs, most of which were offered free.

The Road Scholar program met many goals of our organizational mission. We could travel locally and then internationally to visit art galleries, enjoy theatre and concerts, architecture and learn about diverse cultures.

Sometimes you have to have a gimmick. After paying their annual membership fee, each member received a card with a row of ten possible punch spaces across the bottom. Every time a member took a domestic Road Scholar bus tour, they received a punch on their membership card. If they had ten punches, they could enjoy the next trip free.

The City of Toronto offered many opportunities for our growing membership to expand their cultural horizons. Eventually, the program offered trips to other North American destinations and to Europe.

Our members love the trips because we not only went to many theatre presentations with orchestra seats, but we also visited art museums for major exhibitions and walked on historical architectural and ethnic neighbourhood tours. Tour goers looked forward to the surprise of opening their box lunches which not only had delicious eatables but were decorated to match the occasion e.g. a cold Asian salad for Miss Saigon, or a red rose atop black and red ribbons for Phantom of the Opera.

Each domestic trip required me to get up very early on a Saturday morning to box the contents of forty-eight lunches, getting the ingredients ready for the Bloody Mary's or Screwdrivers, and making sure that friends could sit with friends on the bus and in the theatre.

Meals were always eaten in interesting and different fine restaurants where many of our participants would not have had the opportunity to go to. More importantly, they were in non-senior properties. In other words, no buffets.

Once in a while, even though I had checked things out ahead of time, there was a glitch which made the occasion memorable. When the AGO in Toronto had an exhibition on the Hermitage Museum in Russia, I found a small restaurant that had Russian cuisine. The owner said he could seat forty-six people with room to spare. Wrong. We squeezed in. The owner banged a large brass gong with the start of each course, but when dessert and coffee were served there were not enough coffee cups. Some of my more adventuresome members got up, went into the kitchen, and started washing dishes.

***

Programs and residencies were used to benefit students at all levels and were spread out all around Niagara County. In presenting these programs, I realized that most of the young people had never experienced a live performance and they had no idea how to sit still and behave during a presentation.

That fact gave me the idea of presenting performances for area adults who were never exposed to any of the many art forms. I scheduled these in small and unexpected alternative settings. Thanks to a three-year grant from Affiliate Artists, a national organization, I was able to place the poet Joan Murray whose work has been published in the Atlantic Monthly, Harpers, Ms., and the New York Times, (remember that third floor elocution room); harpist and graduate of the Julliard School Sally Goodwin (the golden harp behind the curtain); and an actress Kathleen

Gaffney, Co-founder of Artsgenesis Creativity Inc. (make believe me in my youth). They each spent seven weeks, twice daily, to meet and perform for people of all ages in motor pools, malls, parks, nursing homes, YMCA's, coffee shops, juvenile detention settings, granges, VFW halls and more. The poetry produced by the young women at Lockport's Center for Unwed Mothers was both sincere and emotional. Presenting these programs were all very wonderful, and for me, personally rewarding.

I wrote and received two grants from the National Endowment of the Arts, which in turn, were then used for capital projects including a new foundation under the historic "Das Haus" in Wheatfield, a roof on a piece of the carousel portion of the Carousel Museum in North Tonawanda, and a portion of the roof for one of the buildings at Old Fort Niagara in Youngstown. The Endowment also funded an Architectural program designed by me and led by Robert Shibley, Dean of the University of Buffalo School of Architecture in three Niagara County Middle Schools. My hope was that these students would forever view and appreciate the great architectural styles and treasures found in Western New York. Both federal grants required enormous amounts of paperwork, both during, mid-way and after the end of the projects. At the time, I believe that the Niagara Council of the Arts was the only arts organization in Western New York to receive two NEA grants in a row. Only seven Architecture grants were given to organizations across the United States that year. A real coup.

***

Niagara County needed any or all art forms which could and would enhance the education, recreation and especially the tourism profile of the community. My aim was to change all that, and over the course of thirty years I explored and offered many programs. Primary was our ongoing ArtWheels classes for children at our Art Center which operated twelve months a year. Twice we acquired a truck through a member item from New York State and Assemblyman Joseph Pillittere in order to offer a mobile version of ArtWheels. Four certified art teachers presented free art classes in ten Niagara County parks during the eight weeks of summer. This program was successful for 22 years. Program expenses for ArtWheels came from a number of sources. The Niagara County Legislature and the Niagara County Youth Bureau were major funding sources.

When the arts council acquired the Carnegie building there was no art gallery in the city and few in the County. I began exhibitions with the help of the Smithsonian and Gallery Associates of New York State (GANYS), both of whom loaned excellent travelling shows. These shows were placed mostly in bank lobbies, but sometimes in schools and even in the lobby of the Niagara Falls City Hall. This helped to establish a rapport with the banks who would later be asked for financial support. Since I was in a building owned by the city, I always needed maintenance support from city hall. I also needed the schools to cooperate when I presented educational programs.

***

One of the first art exhibitions I presented in the rotunda of the Carnegie building were works by the then popular Leroy Neiman, whose prints of sports figures were all the rage at the time. To this day in Niagara Falls, nothing is as popular as sports except casinos, so I knew it would be well received. The opening took place on a hot, steamy day in July. With no air conditioning, all of the historic, long two-storied wooden windows were lifted up as high as they would go. There were no screens. The swinging front entrance doors were propped open to establish a bit of a breeze. The turnout was wonderful. People came because they were either curious, loved sports or the artist Leroy Neiman or maybe both. All the local politicians attended. Sam was as proud as a peacock because WE had pulled this off.

Since the entrance doors were wide open, it was an invitation to come in. I noticed an unusual looking couple coming up the marble stairs. The word hippie seems appropriate. The young male and female looked exactly alike with jean pants and jackets, long straight greasy hair and the look of needing a square meal. I walked over to introduce myself and offer them some refreshments. The young man spoke to me in French. My history of speaking French at a young age kicked in. He said that he and his girlfriend were touring the country. I told them to enjoy the artwork and then moved away. A very short time later the City Manager Harvey Albond came over to me to tell me that the girl seemed ill. I brought the girl into my office, gave her a glass of water, a comfortable chair and told her to rest.

I returned to the attendees. Once more, Harvey came over to me to say that the same young lady was now lying on the ground, outside next to the driveway. I went out to see her and decided she needed hospital care. It seemed that while viewing the show, she had been bitten on the ear lobe by a bee. She was in shock.

I drove her and her partner to the emergency room. When she was being examined, her friend told me she was expectant, and they had no money or any place to stay that night. He said that his father was sending him money via Western Union the next day. What could I do? I said that they could stay at our house until they could get settled.

Jim Allen was not the soul of tolerance, so he wasn't at all happy to welcome the two God d- - - hippies. I explained the situation. The next day I took the pair to get the young man's money at Western Union. Then I stopped at the local health food store to get certain health foods that the young lady said she needed.

When I went downstairs the next morning, the house reeked of a foul sour wheat smell. Henri had a pot of gruel sputtering on the kitchen stove for his beloved. Jim Allen typical morning routine was ruined. I had to get the pair out of our house. Henri needed work and they needed a place to stay. Since Niagara County is a fruit belt, I found them a job picking apples, and they stayed right there in the barn of a Niagara County farm. Five months later I received a letter from Vancouver, Canada. The couple had crossed the country, and now, just as she was about to give birth, Henri had disappeared. There was a return address, so my daughters and I put together and sent a complete layette. A year later, she wrote to me again, this time from France, and thanked us for our kindness.

The Niagara Power Project brought the population of the city up to 102,000 residents in 1960. It then began to decline. The mayor at the time, Mayor E. Dent Lackey, was a believer in what most people thought was an ill-conceived, federally-aided Urban Renewal project that decimated most of the downtown area, tearing down all of the buildings within 10 blocks of the Falls.

In its place, a centerpiece Convention Center designed by Philip Johnson was built in 1973 which could accommodate 10,000 people. It would have the largest amount of continuous floor space in any Convention Center in the country. It was fronted by a block-long cement plaza with a wooden semi-circular seating area at one end, a couple of fountains, and an underground piping system to make surface ice in the wintertime which seldom worked. At the upper level of the plaza behind the seating area was a trailer which was intended to house sound equipment. Even though the seating area did not have a stage, every event was under the jurisdiction of the Convention Centers' Stagehands Union. A red carpeted underground tunnel led from the Convention Center, under the plaza, and led to a glass alley which was supposed to front small boutique stores between the Convention Center and the Falls. That plan never materialized. Because the plaza had multiple levels of brick walkways, it was necessary to put in dozens of staircases. When built, the lip of each stair was edged in brass. All stair railings were aluminum and had internal lighting.

The space was in a kind of limbo. Who was in charge? Was it the Director of the Convention Center, the Director of City Parks and Recreation Department or who? In the summer of 1976 I took over the outdoor space by eminent domain. I didn't ask, I just did it. The outdoor space now had the Niagara Council of the Arts as a tenant and I would now give the locals and tourists something to do on a hot summer night.

The programs were free and were called the Niagara Summer Experience. Although the space had a seating area, it had no stage. The city was generous in building us a stage, but they didn't communicate with me before it was started and partly built. The completed platform was too high, with no means to enter or exit stage right or stage left. Stairs behind the stage allowed performers to awkwardly go on and off of the stage. A step too close to the front could result in a disastrous fall on the cement far below. We warned all of the performers and somehow, we made it work.

I used the same format for the next twenty-two years. All programs were free and took place on the Saturdays and Sundays of July and August. Early on I realized that I couldn't do it alone. I soon found out that the more you involve and partner with other organizations, the more successful the program. Others made me look good. My hope was that each program would have some educational value disguised as an evening of fun. Other than the Falls themselves, it gave the tourists something to do.

I have a vivid memory of the first Summer Experience program in 1976. Months before, I met with the pastor and his lovely wife of the Antiochian Orthodox Church. We planned to have a Lebanese Experience with traditional food stuff, Lebanese music played on traditional Arabic instruments and communal dancing. The ladies of the church could keep all of the profits of their food sales. I knew many of the dedicated church ladies and I was confident that they could pull the program off. I explained to Father A. that I knew someone who might accept an invitation to perform as the headline artist. Her name was Tullah Hanley, the woman who was Father O'Heron's 'Merry Widow' of Bradford, PA. I had remembered her from years before. There was a lot of publicity regarding the opening evening of a new series of events which would take place in the always empty downtown.

I signed a contract with Ms. Hanley. She was to meet me in front of the plaza at 4 p.m., after which I would take her to her hotel. She would perform at 8 p.m.

It was a brilliant day and by 4 p.m. the plaza space was buzzing with activity. I had asked Mayor O'Laughlin and the City Manager Don O'Hara to greet Ms. Hanley when she arrived. I had my daughter Joan in tow. Shortly after the appointed time, a car pulled up chauffeured by a young, rosy cheeked boy who did not even look old enough to drive. As she emerged from the back seat, two long and very bare legs swung out of the car. She stood up in her platform six-inch stiletto heels to reveal a very skimpy skirt that barely covered her private parts. Her belt was made of brass links which held two cupped brass hands dangling down and inward, one from the front and the other from the back. As she walked, those hands caressed her body. I felt a need to cover my daughter Joan's eyes with my hands. The two city officials were speechless. I should have known then and there that there would be more problems to follow.

The two incredulous men made a quick getaway and I drove Tullah to her hotel. When we got her to her room, I offered to take her out for dinner. She declined showing both of us the inside of her small suitcase where five cobs of corn, still in their husks, were waiting to be eaten raw. I told her that her performance tonight was sponsored by a church and that it was a family event. In other words, don't give me any grief. I'd see her in the dressing room at 7:30 p.m.

At the appointed time I met her in the dressing room. She had a kimono /bathrobe over her dress. I went back outside and viewed the crowd. There was not a space facing the plaza stage that didn't have people sitting, standing or hanging. The makeshift sound trailer had so many young people on the roof that it was swaying precariously. There were thousands of people. It seemed that downtown Niagara Falls was reborn.

At 8 p.m. I walked onto the stage, took the microphone, and began by thanking all of the entities that made this new series, and this program in particular, possible. As I introduced Ms. Hanley, her taped traditional music began with the jingles of the *riq*, a tambourine-like musical instrument. Then out came Tullah, whose body undulated with each note. There was a momentary hush, then the crowd stirred and gasped. Tullah had nary a stitch on beneath her sheer white kaftan, made even more evident by the back spotlighting. It all happened so fast.

The newly appointed Convention Center Director Lou Harp with his deep southern accent yelled, "God damn, get that woman off of my stage."

Father yelled, "Tell them she's not from our church".

I ran mid-stage to drag her to the side. I told her that she could not continue unless she put something on. She refused, went into the dressing room to get her driver and left. The musicians that the church had hired took her place on stage and the program continued without incident. What could top that for the opener of a new series!

***

I hoped that the programs would be entertaining but also have an educational aspect for these audiences who seldom traveled. Many of them were narrow minded and poorly educated. Each of the festivals was an education for me. I learned to understand and treat each ethnic group with respect and patience as I found each ethnic group to be very different. Without exception, the Lebanese women were always sweet, kind and good.

There is a large Polish community in our area, and their special day was always well received and well attended. During the winter months the Polish community initiated traditional dance classes for their young people who would then perform in the plaza the following summer. They fundraised during the year so that their dancers could buy authentic lavishly embroidered costumes from Poland. The hardworking women baked and cooked for weeks. All I had to do was bring in the Polka bands. I never knew how much profit they made because they were always extremely secretive when counting their money. Their quiet, 'I know something you don't know' smiles always told me that their day was a financial success.

I tried to keep things fresh and interesting. We had a Scottish Experience which we began by ceremoniously carrying in a haggis, with bagpipes playing all the while. Colorful Country Dancers performed with swords, whirling their traditional kilts. I presented Balkan dancers whose interesting costumes included soft leather laced slippers with curled up toes. American Cloggers also proved that shoes were what their program was all about.

Every year we had an Irish night sponsored by the local Hibernian Association. Several small Irish bands played during the evening with lots of dancing and lots of hooting and yelling. And lots of beer. Kegs and kegs were consumed. If beer was being served I always planned with Certo, the local beer distributor, to come at 1 a.m. the following morning and remove the beer truck. Close to that time, the Hibernians would use 16-ounce paper cups to empty another keg, and line those cups along a plaza's concrete ledge. The truck would leave but the party would continue. At 3 a.m. I would lock the bathrooms and turn out all of the plaza lights. I always wondered how they could drive home.

We had Native American Experiences, usually with a sparse audience. The colorful costumed dancers were always late and didn't seem to care about time, place or space. They just side-stepped to the beat of their music and fervently sang their traditional songs.

***

The five local Italians societies were cantankerous from the very beginning. Their annual planning meetings, which lasted all year round, were loud and argumentative. Who would sell pepper and onions this year? Who would sell lemon ice because the profit margin was so high? Where would their booth be located? Why would we have that band when this band was better? Did I mention patience?

The Folk Arts division of the New York State Council of the Arts took note of the programs, and wanted to fund something authentic, something educational, traditional and interesting. One year they suggested a Calabrian family group from the Smithsonian who sang centuries-old mountain songs. The planning group of Italians were not impressed but because I wanted to be in good graces with NYSCA I planned for the family to come and share their traditional music with the locals. Many press releases beforehand explained the group's notable background and accomplishments.

Early on that Saturday evening our Calabrian mama began on the microphone with a high-pitched lament, while the rest of the family accompanied her on the tambourine and accordion. No one stopped eating or even looked up. I guess the attendees had missed the press releases because they wondered where those people came from and why the ear shattering high range singing. Everyone rolled their eyes. On the other hand, when the band from Toronto started to play, everyone smiled and began to dance.

# HICKSVILLE

Niagara Falls had a fairly large population of African Americans. As many people and as many organizations as I knew, I could not find a community partner with any church or organization. I really tried, not only because I thought it was very important, but because NYSCA was pushing me. I decided to ask NYSCA to fund a performance by the amazing duo Ossie Davis and Ruby Dee. The State came up with the money. I advertised this particular free event all over Western New York. Locally I used the bulletins of every little church to get the word out. I used traditional press and our summer brochure. It was on a Saturday, and when I arrived on the scheduled day in the late afternoon, the plaza was empty. Soon the stagehands arrived to set the sound and the lights. Programs always started at 8 p.m. Around 5 p.m. the plaza began to fill up with young boys, not the families that I had hoped for. More and more boys arrived, all between the ages of about thirteen and eighteen. No females, no adults black or white, no supervision. The audience came from Buffalo by Metro bus and by car. Most of the young men had a boom box perched on their shoulder and were moving to that particular rhythm. While the performance took place, the audience stood below the performers with their backs to the stage. The 'audience' were all talking, yelling or just not paying attention to what was happening on the stage. It became difficult to hear the presentation. The famous duo had a female Japanese manager. She told me that they had travelled all over the world for many years and had never seen such a situation. She was truly disgusted with Niagara Falls. When Ms. Dee and Mr. Davis left the stage there was nary a clap. They just left and so did I.

Very early the next morning I had an ominous feeling and so I went back to the plaza. I enjoyed photography, so I always had a camera in my car. I was shocked at the condition of the plaza, so I took photographs. Latrines were ripped off of the wall, toilets clogged with whole rolls of paper, outdoor chairs thrown into the water of the fountains. Trash was everywhere. The police department always sent a couple of officers to patrol each event. The police chief told me that he had been informed about the number of young people and he sent extra officers. They were told not to go into the plaza itself.

Programming for the following year did not have an African American component. A gentleman from the Buffalo NAACP made an appointment with me to protest. I showed him the pictures and that was that. To this day I have no idea how this all happened but from that day on I made a concerted effort to partner with Niagara County schools and churches to present meaningful African American cultural programs in a wide variety of settings. I bought a set of traditional African drums and hired drummers to perform in all of the County parks and have children participate.

NYSCA also wanted me to program something Hispanic but much to their chagrin, we had a zero Hispanic population. However, I did present a small troupe from the Ballet Hispanico in New York City to a very small audience.

As a NYSCA panelist, I became good friends with Alan Chow who was the Executive Director of the Chinese American Arts Council in Manhattan. He was also the Artistic Director of the Chinese American Dance Company in New York City. He and his company drove to Niagara Falls in a beat-up bus to present a wonderful and colorful music and dance experience on the plaza. The problem was that the housing they had anticipated did not work out. I invited the twenty of them to spend the night on my living room floor. My girls still talk about the time they came home late only to step over our impromptu Asian visitors who were exhausted and were sleeping in a scattered pattern on our living room floor.

***

Big band nights included the Duke Ellington Orchestra, the Glenn Miller Orchestra, the Stan Kenton Orchestra, the Buddy Rich Orchestra and the Les Elgart Orchestra. Mr. Elgart and his lovely wife joined me for dinner. What a classy and loving couple. The audience loved to dance under the stars to the familiar rhythms of the big band sound and imagine, it was all for free. New York State would not fund any of these bands because they were too common.

A very elderly Mr. Kenton went on stage accompanied by an older woman described as his manager. She led him to the piano bench, helped him sit down and then placed his two hands on the keys. He died the next week. Could it have been something in our water?

On the evening that Buddy Rich and his orchestra performed, he got on the microphone after the first number. The audience had already moved into the space in front of the stage to dance. He announced that this was a concert and not suitable for dancing.

He added, "This must be Hicksville".

People didn't pay attention and continued to dance. My custom was to go to the dressing room at intermission to present the performers with their check. When they returned to the stage, they played one set and in unison got up and left, much to the disappointment of the large crowd.

On Monday morning I called the American Federation of Musicians in New York to tell them we intended to sue. We got our money back and the person I spoke to in that office said that this was nothing new, Buddy was a real a jerk.

The annual jazz nights included performances by jazz greats George Shearing and a superior Marian McPartland. They were both outstanding.

***

There were so many area performing arts groups that I didn't have to look far for suitable and delightful entertainment. Included in the series was a night for Square Dancers who came from all over Western New York and Canada for their special annual event. Country Western, Barbershoppers, Sweet Adelines, local theatre groups, church choirs and on and on were all presented. Each kind of performance brought its own audience to add to the mix of regulars.

Among the regulars was a small group of people who lived in a halfway house about a half a mile away. They were led by a very short, bow-legged man, about forty years old, holding the hand of a scraggly young girl of about fifteen. Mex always wore an extra-large black cowboy hat adorned with a long dirty sea gull feather. They always arrived early and sat in the very front row of the curved wooden seating. One night in the middle of a performance someone ran up to me and said to come quick. They pointed to Mex and his young friend who were laying across the bench on top of each other, and going at it hot and heavy. I ran down and poked him.

"Mex, you can't do that in public. Stop." I yelled above the music.

"OK, Jacquie" he replied nasally as he rolled off of her.

That night the audience got a show within a show, and from then on, I paid special attention to Mex and his followers. The exception was the night that the Hibernians saved all of those free glasses of beer. Mex and his friends imbibed with the Hibernians and were still there when I left for home.

In 1984 I signed a contract with a fledgling Montreal-based group called Cirque du Soleil. Today they are headliners in Las Vegas! We presented the Swingle Singers, an eight-voice a cappella jazz group whose singers had performed all over the world. There was no admission for the programs on the plaza, so after their first number a third of the audience just got up and left. They didn't understand the non-instrument performance. Both of these groups were paid for by the State.

***

Each year we had an event called *KidFest* as a part of the summer series. We partnered with many area agencies whose mission involved children. The event was filled with games, colorful events and professional theatre presentations designed for young children.

The nearby Village of Lewiston had a successful chalk walk every year as a part of their annual Art Show. Their program was always so well received and always garnered a wide range of PR. One year I decided to try a Chalk Walk at *KidFest*. When I found out how expensive chalk was, I asked the Carborundum Company to sponsor the event so I could purchase the chalk. There was plenty of cement in the area, on the ground and on all of the surrounding walls of the plaza. It was a bare canvas. Hundreds of children arrived that week-end. I had enough staff and volunteers to supervise and distribute the chalk. Young participants had a wonderful time creating lots of rainbows, flowers, ice cream cones and pictures of family members.

On Monday morning at 8 a.m. I arrived at my office located at the top of that same plaza. I was surprised to see a fire truck and two city cars parked next to the curb. The firemen explained that they were told to hose all of the children's art works away. The next day I received a letter on city stationery from a City Department head. The letter claimed that I was teaching children how to deface public property. Included was a bill for Spick and Span and the cost of the firemen. I paid the bill under protest and could only feel sorry for a person, a city department head, with such stupidity.

# FRANCIS

My affair with Sam was not what it once was. He was involved in many of the Art Councils programs and still felt that he could control my life. Then an unexpected and unlikely person came into my life. It was a person whom I shall call Francis.

Since my children were getting older, many times I would go back to my office after dinner to be alone and concentrate on putting together a grant application, always just under the deadline. There were too many interruptions during the day in the office and too noisy and distracting at home. On one such evening in 1978, I was writing away when the phone rang. It was Francis who said he was in town and would like to meet with me tonight to discuss a collaboration of his company with one of our programs. We had worked together on a few Niagara County projects. I said I was alone and working late, so just bang on the front door so I could let him in. And bang he did.

Francis was one of the wealthiest businessmen in Western New York. His headquarters were in Buffalo and he had the respect of every executive and politician in the area. He sat on many prestigious Boards of Directors. He was interesting because he liked many of the same things that I did. I knew he had a lovely wife and family, and that he was much older than I, so his sudden interest in me came as a complete and, I mean complete, shock.

Over the next seven years our relationship continued and grew as trusted best friends more than anything physical. I think he liked my company because he felt comfortable with me, could trust me and I was a good listener. Just like in the movies, he had a long-time secretary by the name of Lucy, who controlled total access to her boss. She liked me, so my calls were always put right through and we became very good friends. She relayed the where and when of many Buffalo supper dates. Francis was so well known that it forced me to always take a yellow pad and pencil to the restaurant table, so it would look like I had some business with him. After dinner we would make our way back to each of our families. He would tell me when he just wanted to think. When he needed silence, I would drive his car for a couple of hours along the Lake Erie shore in silence.

We traveled together often, he in First Class and me in Coach, which never bothered me. His secretary made all of the arrangements. I tagged along when he had business in New York City. We always stayed at the Essex on Central Park south. Once we were coming down the stairs together to return to the airport and home, when the politician Ned Reagan came up the stairs and spied Francis. He came over to greet him, while I just slid by, took my own taxi and reconnected at the airport.

Once I went with him to Boston because he had business there. It was a hot sticky August evening when we caught a cab to our hotel. As we traveled from the airport, Francis said he felt dizzy. He leaned on me in the back seat. We got to the hotel and the doorman helped me get him onto a chair in the lobby. Lucy had made all of the arrangements, so it was an easy check in. We went upstairs, and he still looked awfully pale and he said he still felt ill. He got into bed and I sat on the chair. He said he thought it was his heart which wasn't in the best shape. It was late, but I called the hotel manager and asked him to come up. I declared that I was not Mrs. Francis but I needed his help. A doctor was summoned, who said Francis should go home immediately. I called Lucy who got him on a very early morning flight to Buffalo and made arrangements for someone to be waiting there to pick him up. I took him by cab to Logan Airport at the crack of dawn, got him on the plane and returned back to the hotel where I stayed until I went back to airport that night. I expected the worse. As soon as I landed in Buffalo I called Lucy who said that when he arrived he demanded to go straight to his office, that he was working and that he was just fine.

He did have health issues. His doctor suggested that it would be good for his heart, his weight and his cholesterol if he would follow the most current health plan by a famous doctor, whose diet book was on the New York Times Bestseller Top Ten list for 54 weeks. Francis made a reservation to stay for two weeks at the clinic located on the Santa Monica beach right next to the ocean waves.

Now, as it happens, my mother Blanche lived very close by. I flew out to California and stayed with her during his second week stay. Every night he would check himself out and I would pick him up in my mother's older canary yellow Ford Mustang convertible. We would go to the best restaurants and park among a gaggle of expensive luxury cars. Francis was able to enjoy vichyssoise instead of cabbage soup.

He wanted to take me to Quebec City, so I could stay in the hotel where my mother was a chambermaid. It was wonderful until, on the return flight home in Montreal, someone recognized me in the Montreal airport. They told my husband Jim Allen, but he never had a reaction.

I wanted to see Europe, so he managed to take me to Europe, I loved violets, so Francis gave me a crate of mixed colors. I loved fine wine and he sent me a case of the best French Grand Cru wines. Oh, how I wish I had saved some of those bottles before gulping them down. He was always so very sweet. I never fooled myself. I knew we could never have more than an ideal friendship.

If you are doing the math, that year there were now three men in my life, my uninterested husband Jim, controlling Sam and my dear sweet friend Francis.

***

1978 was a year that I remember well for another reason. I was working in my office on a spring day in May when the phone rang. It was a girl "Q" who had dated Tim when they were in high school. Tim lived at home and had moved on from that long past relationship with "Q". He had a good job in Buffalo and was now engaged to a charming young lady in a nearby community.

The girl on the phone asked if I could meet her for lunch because she had something important to tell me. I met her the next day and she announced that she was pregnant with Tim's child. I was flabbergasted. I went home that night and talked to Tim. He said that a couple of months before, "Q" had called him to visit her because she was having a problem. Out of past friendship, he visited her to see if he could help her. He insisted that it could not be his child. She insisted that it was. As a result, he broke his engagement, and tried to be supportive to "Q".

Close to the time that the baby was due, still insisting it could not be his child, he left for California and his Grandmother Blanche's house.

***

It was in the early fall of that year that same year when I walked past Wakes, the best men's store in Niagara Falls. The most beautiful beige cashmere topcoat was softly draped over the shoulders of the mannequin in the window. I thought how handsome Jim would look in that coat. I could buy it on a time plan. Just before Christmas I made the final payment, Wakes wrapped the box and added a big red bow. I put his gift under the tree with all of the children's presents.

On Christmas morning I got up early to make a special holiday breakfast. Soon the whole family gathered around the tree to open their presents. I hurried back into the kitchen after I realized that Jim had not given me a present. I started to cry. He came in to see how breakfast was coming and asked me what the matter was. I told him I was disappointed that he didn't buy me a present.

His answer was, "Didn't you buy something for yourself a couple of months ago on the credit card".

That morning, while stirring the omelets, I made a decision to begin a new life. I set the date of April 15, 1979 to leave with the three girls. Tim was already in California and the other two boys could stay with Jim in the house.

During the next few months I put my plan into action. I applied and received two credit cards in my name since I had little resources.

***

The following February on an evening when we were experiencing a wild Western New York blizzard, the phone rang. It was "Q" asking if son John would get her to the hospital. And he did, God bless him. I made up my mind on that snowy evening that I would never try to see that baby since I knew that I would fall in love with the child who would be my first grandchild. My marriage was broke, and so was I. I didn't need any other complication in my life.

I saved a bit of money and put a deposit on a very small apartment in nearby Lewiston. It had a view of the Niagara River, and I thought that would have a calming effect on my life. The apartment was so small that poor Judy had to sleep on a pull-out bed for her first year at Niagara University.

April 15th arrived. I gathered the three girls and two suitcases and went to the side door. Jim asked me where I was going, and I told him I was leaving him. He didn't act shocked or surprised! He didn't beg me to stay as I secretly hoped he would. If he had I might have stayed. His only concern was the fact that he would not be able to pay the mortgage.

My first few weeks in that rented apartment were a blur. I felt so guilty that I had broken up and disrupted each of my children's lives. Two suitcases were not enough to keep the three girls and me outfitted. After a couple of weeks, I made a short list of things that I needed from the house in Niagara Falls. In hindsight, I wished I had been more astute in what I left behind. Just like after a fire or a flood, there are things that you can't replace. When I graduated from St. Joseph's College, the principal, Sister St. Stephan, signed and gave me a book called "the Imitation of Christ". I'm not sure why but that book meant a lot to me. Over the years I've thought of many things including that book, and I always felt a sense of regret and loss.

I asked one of my sons if he and a some of his friends could bring me the items on the list, including the contents of my dresser. I thought that they brought everything on the list. The next day I realized that my diamond ring was missing from the top dresser drawer. I asked my son if one of his friends could have taken it, and the answer was "no", but I wasn't so sure.

I drove to Main Street to the only local pawn shop in town and asked the owner if anyone had brought in a gold ring which contained four large diamonds. He, too, said no, so I went to the police. It only took the detectives five minutes to have one of the boys admit that he had stolen the ring. I did not press charges because I knew his wonderful parents who were so penitent. They promised that their teenage son would earn the money to have the diamonds reset. The ring's gold setting and the four diamonds, neatly wrapped in folded white tissue paper, were returned by the pawnbroker and the diamonds were reinserted into the prongs. Several years later I was throwing in a load of wash into a coin machine when one of the diamonds dislodged from the setting and went down the drain with the water.

My marriage to Jim Allen was also down the drain. On July 22, 1981, we quietly divorced.

***

Four years later in 1983, Tim still remained in California, had begun a successful career as an Engineer with Boeing. His two brothers had moved to California too.

At Christmas time that year, the local YWCA, located just a short distance from the Carnegie building, was going to close its doors after many years of service. I had read that the staff had planned a holiday farewell luncheon. I was busy with piles of paperwork, and in the morning, I decided not to go. Before lunchtime, something told me to take a break, go down the street and say goodbye to this wooden monument of Niagara's past. I needed lunch anyhow.

I sat by myself in the back of the auditorium. The Director got on the microphone to announce that the children from the "Y" daycare would be coming out to sing Christmas songs. A group of four-year old preschoolers formed a crooked line on the stage and each child seemed to have that Mediterranean look. Right in the middle of the line was a very skinny and very pale blue-eyed toe-head, who looked remarkably like Tim. I did the math. I walked over to the piano player, my heart thumping, and asked her what the blonde boy's name was, and of course, you guessed it, "Q" was his mother. I almost collapsed. I started to cry just thinking that this youngster was my first grandchild.

I felt such guilt. I called “Q” that evening and told her that anything the boy needed, I would supply. And then it started. As the boy grew up, he called me many times for things like a special bike or a leather football jacket. There was never any doubt that Tim was his father, because after all, I had many pictures to compare the two of them taken at the same age.

When the boy was sixteen, he called me. He said he wanted to know his father. Maybe I could blame my sentimental reaction in the Christmas season, but I gave him Tim’s work telephone number.

I got a call from California two weeks later. It was Tim and he was very, very upset. That day he had appeared in front of an Orange County judge who demanded he pay back support for “Q’s” child. He told the judge that he was not the father. The judge ordered a DNA test for Tim, “Q” and the boy. The results came back that Tim was not the father, and it seems “Q” knew it all along. For all that I did with love and sincerity, and all that I gave to my “grandson” over those years, the boy or his mother never contacted me again. He just disappeared like a wave of water hitting the sand. Now I have the distinction of being an ex-grandmother. How could I have doubted that Tim was telling the truth all along. Mea culpa….

# PAVAROTTI

My job gave me the opportunity to meet many people, especially since I was very involved with two New York State organizations, NYSCA and the Alliance of NYS Arts Councils. I travelled to Albany, the State capitol, at least once a year to advocate increased funding for the arts. Not only did I meet many legislators, but I found myself in the company of many notable artists from all of the disciplines. Among those was a condescending and superior Tony Randall, actor Mickey Rooney who felt sorry for me because I was from Buffalo, lovely Patricia McBride, principal ballerina of the New York City Ballet, a frumpy Martha Stewart who wore old nylons with black crooked seams down the back, wearing a very used jacket with a leopard collar that looked like it had mange, and Kitty Carlisle, who served as Chairman of the New York State Council of the Arts for twenty years. She was an actress and wife of the Pulitzer Prize-winning playwright Moss Hart, and she was a class act.

I was in her company on a number of occasions. She always looked perfect in every way. She wore a classic little black suit with a white under-blouse, a single strand of pearls with earrings to match, nude nylons and black suede opera pumps. Every strand of her dark hair was always in place, and many times a day she applied her ruby red lipstick. I was in Rye, New York, before she was going to go on the stage to speak. Beforehand, she told our small group that she felt very ill and she looked it. Just before she climbed onto the stage she pulled out and applied that ruby lipstick, fixed a smile on her face, and wowed the crowd. She was a pro and she knew. She demanded respect from all who surrounded her.

She knew my face as a member of that Alliance Board, but that was it. I asked her if she could come upstate to the Niagara Council of the Arts 25th annual meeting in upstate New York. She said yes and during the next few weeks I made the arrangements.

The meeting was scheduled on a weekday for a noon luncheon. I gave myself plenty of time to get to the Buffalo airport to meet Mrs. Hart, a name she used instead of her stage name. In order to get to that airport one must drive over Grand Island, New York, which is connected to the mainland by two long high bridges. I hired a limo and off we went. We got over the first bridge when suddenly the traffic came to a dead stop. I watched the time tick by. I convinced the driver to make an illegal cut across the median and go back over the bridge then take the long way around. The skies turned dark and it began to pour. I was thirty minutes late. No cell phones then to let her know.

The driver pulled over to the curb on the far side of the arrivals entrance and handed me a black umbrella. I ran in to find Mrs. Hart sitting alone in a small room. She was fuming mad. I tried to explain as we went to the arrivals level. It was still pouring when we got to the exit of the airport. The limo was waiting across on the other side of the one-way road. I opened the umbrella and pointed to the car.

She said, "you don't expect me to walk over there in the rain, do you?"

I walked back across the street and told the driver to go down a level and come back up closer to the entrance. I kept thinking about all of the attendees who were waiting at the hotel for us. Finally, we were in the limo and on our way. She sat straight as a dye on the far side of the seat. For a while we were both quiet and then I told her about the thruway accident, and how my daughter was having trouble finding school shoes. I told her about our programs for children, and as we drove on, the chill slowly disappeared. We pulled up to the hotel, she applied her ruby red lipstick, and all was well.

***

I never considered getting anyone's autograph and I had lots of opportunities to do so, except for one, that of Luciano Pavarotti.

In the fall of 1979 I received a phone call from Armand Castellani, owner of the TOPS Supermarkets. He explained to me that his sister was dying and that her last wish was that, as an opera devotee, she could meet Luciano Pavarotti. He asked me if I would meet with Michael Bielski, the co-Executive Director of the Buffalo Philharmonic Orchestra and himself, to see if it would be possible to get the famous opera singer to Buffalo. He told us that if that happened and if a concert could take place, the Orchestra and the Art Council would split the profit.

I called everyone I knew in New York City because of my connection to the New York State Council of the Arts. Neither Mr. Bielski or I was successful.

A strike of the New York Opera company finally allowed us to contact Mr. Pavarotti's agent for a concert on September 28, 1980 at Kleinhans Music Hall. A contract, signed by both parties, can contain a number of things such as what food and drink should be in the dressing room, what make and style of piano with tuning instructions, hotel accommodations and other requests of the artist(s). Mr. P's contract requests were interesting. He would be in the area for two days, so he would need accommodations, a female companion (nice way of putting it) while in Buffalo, a steak dinner for him and his companion after the performance and before a reception given at the home of the President of the University of Buffalo. The reception was for VIP's and for those who bought the most expensive tickets. I received an invitation.

All 2,900 seat were sold within 24 hours, and at the last minute additional seating was added in the orchestra pit and on the stage at $1,000 each.

His area host for the two days in Buffalo was Robert Gioia of the Gioia Macaroni Company, chairman of the BPO board. After a tour of his factory, Mr. Gioia was stunned at the singer's request to go horseback riding. The portly guest was soon whisked to the estate of industrialist Franz Stone in East Aurora, New York, where he was fitted with riding gear, and given a horse named Iron Butterfly.

As Pavarotti and his contracted companion (he called her his secretary!) rode through the pastures, the young woman fell off of her horse, bloodied her head and was taken to Buffalo General Hospital in an ambulance accompanied by Pavarotti. She had suffered a concussion and stayed overnight for observation.

The next evening the singer, accompanied only by pianist John Wustman, gave an unforgettable one-hour concert especially enjoyed by Mr. Castellani's sister who had earlier been wheeled into the front row to receive her dying wish. The venue was peppered by cheers and shouts of "Bravo" and many curtain calls. Those of us who had invitations to the UB President's home left Kleinhans Music Hall to drive a short distance away to meet the star. While we stood jammed into every nook and cranny of the lower floor, Luciano was dining with his companion on the upper level. We all waited, waited and waited. About midnight, an upper door opened, and as he came down the grand staircase alone, he waved and twirled his signature white hanky. He had a wide, toothy grin (hummm). Many of us had our invitation and a pen in hand, and as he inched by, I shoved my arm out for his autograph, which was written as a large P and a wavy line.

For many years the profits from that remarkable concert were placed in a special Niagara Council of the Arts fund called "the Pavarotti Fund". It was only used for cash flow and as soon as we received a grant, the money was replaced.

# THE WINTERGARDEN

In 1979 the Niagara Falls Chamber of Commerce organized a small group of like-minded individuals to plan a celebration to enhance the tourism profile of the city during the slow winter months. The Niagara Council of the Arts played an important role in the success of the forty-four day festival. A Festival of Lights, which began in 1980, featured lighted indoor and outdoor displays in the downtown area. I took on the task of decorating and programming the Wintergarden for the festival and continued to do so until the festival's demise after twenty years in the downtown area. It closed because of lack of both corporate sponsorship and volunteers. Some fresh ideas, especially partnered with new technologies, and new leadership, could have breathed new life into a tired program. In Niagara Falls, Ontario, their Festival of Lights, after thirty years, has emerged as one of the top winter tourist multipliers in Canada.

"A Festival of Lights" was the perfect time to get people into the much maligned building. For each of those years I organized and attended sixty-six school and community group performances in the Wintergarden. School and church choirs, musical groups and their families from all around Western New York looked forward to coming to Niagara Falls to participate. For many, it became an annual ritual.

Before I continue, I have to explain about the Niagara Falls Wintergarden. It was built in 1977 and was designed by the world-class architect Cesar Pelli. It was featured on the cover of Life Magazine, Progressive Architecture and the Architectural Record. It was an angled glass arboretum with a wide variety of 7,000 tropical plants and trees intersected by raised walkways and small waterfalls built with slate from the Niagara Gorge. The Wintergarden included a small, intimate space ideal for poetry readings, small performance groups, and most of all small weddings. I thought the building and the space inside were forward thinking and wonderful. Unfortunately, I was very much in the minority. Three years earlier I was proud that our community was home to the new Earl Brydges Library designed by the internationally famous Paul Rudolph. The building taxed the soul of most local residents.

This architectural jewel was neglected from the very beginning. The atrium contained hundreds of plants and trees; all needed professional horticultural care. The city didn't budget for this kind of care, but relied on a sincere and hardworking Paul, a young man from the Parks Department, who did his very best with no resources.

I always felt that the Wintergarden was a special and unique space for our community. Once when I was on a sightseeing bus in Berlin, Germany, one of our first stops was their "Wintergarden" a reuse of a train station. As we entered soft music was playing over a loud speaker while local residents sat sipping coffee and reading their newspapers. A group of people were engrossed in Tai Chi. The building was a part of their quality of life.

I thought of Niagara Falls, New York, and all of the possibilities that our local building could bring, especially with regards to tourism which was pathetic compared to our neighbours across the river.

Because it was built with federal (HUD) dollars, it didn't matter if the Christian Christmas was being celebrated, the decor and music could not reflect any religious theme. That is why I was very careful that all of the decorations and public address music would be celebratory but not reflective of any particular faith. In other words, "Silent Night" and "Oh Little Town of Bethlehem" were out much to the displeasure of many attendees. The natural ambiance of the space evoked a feeling of enchantment, so it wasn't difficult to duplicate those feelings by putting together tapes of flute, string, and harp music to be played over the public address system. Hopefully when visitors entered the building, they would be immersed in any holiday theme that I had selected.

I was given a very paltry amount of money from the committee to decorate each year. It became a challenge to see how far imagination could trump fiscal constraints. My youngest daughter Mary Helen's high school art class made Papier Mache monkeys one year. I asked the art teacher if I could have them. I called the Chiquita Banana organization who generously sent me very large yellow cardboard bananas. I paired the two to make an interesting display in one corner of the building. Another year I hung several artificial Christmas trees upside down from the highest section of the glass ceiling. It evoked many, many comments.

My friend Jack Maharian was a wonderful floral designer. One year we teamed up to conjure a dynamite theme. I drove my old battered station wagon twenty miles to the mannequin hospital in downtown Buffalo. We bought twelve figures that were in fairly good condition. We placed them on the seats in the back of my wagon. A few cars honked and gave us the peace sign as they past us on the highway.

The a-sexual plastic bodies were shapeless and hairless. I made them into fairies. I sprayed them with flat gold spray, and then applied spray glue and gold glitter in a graceful wave down their bodies. Large wings made of wire and netting were attached and each mannequin held a wand. I went to the local appliance store and dragged away their largest refrigerator box. I cut it into a flat surface, applied spray glue and rolls of cotton batten, and made a huge cloud. I placed four fairies, each holding a glittering wand topped off by a silver star, onto the top of the cloud and paid the stagehand union to raise the cloud high into the peak of the building.

That year, fairies peeked out from behind bushes and plants, surrounded by artificial large pink cabbage roses and Japanese wooden bird cages. Piped in ethereal flute music played by Jean Pierre Rampal completed the holiday atmosphere.

On the day before the festival I invited two Chamber of Commerce executives to come to the Wintergarden and see our creative display. I was stunned to hear them say that "this is a family affair" and that I would have to cloth the non-male/female fairies before the opening the next day. One was the former

Superintendant of Schools, the other the Executive Director of the Chamber of Commerce.

My answer was, "What? Have you ever seen an art book?".

No matter, they said that the fairies could not be naked.

The next morning, I called the stagehands to lower the cloud, which would incur another union expense. I rushed to a nearby mall to visit a Frederick's of Hollywood store where naughty intimate apparel was sold. I bought twelve see-through gauzy pink and powder blue teddies with snaps in the crotch area. I hurried back to the Wintergarden and dressed each fairy, much to the laughter of the stagehands. They raised the cloud once again. I can only say that what were once beautiful pure objects now became a sexual joke.

The gardens were also used as a setting for weddings, for family portraits, Christmas card subjects, and a place for lovers to sit together in pure contentment. It was a place where rich and poor alike could sit on one of the benches to read a newspaper or book, drink a cup of coffee or eat a bag lunch, or to just find themselves in a place of peace and tranquility. A few sparrows flew through the air and cheeped in their home away from home.

Tourism in Niagara Falls, New York, continued to decline well into the 80's and 90's. On the other hand, Niagara Falls, Ontario, on the other side of the Niagara River, was expanding their tourism horizons, even borrowing the idea of our hokey "A Festival of Lights" and starting a newer, glitzier and more state-of-the-arts program. Their long-term leadership, foresight and creativity propelled them forward in a major way. Our lack of leadership held us back.

***

The years after "A Festival of Lights" were not kind to the Wintergarden. The city sold the property to a Native American business man who converted it into an embarrassing Wintergarden Play Center. Then the 'powers that be' decided that the building should come down because it was an impediment for a direct route from the new casino to the State park. Besides, it was too expensive to maintain it.

In 2007 I visited the City Manager, who told me that the Mayor had a vision for the downtown and it did not include the Wintergarden. I suggested that multilingual signage could direct any tourist through the doors of the building and find the State park straight ahead. I asked the question "should every building sitting astride a public street be torn down for a visual effect?" Europe is full of examples. Perhaps the French should tear down the Arc de Triumph in Paris because it sits in the middle of the Champs-Elysees? How about the Brandenburg Gate in Berlin? Tear it down.

I also suggested that the building be converted to indicate the city's long history of power and electricity and create a new connection to eco-tourism. There could be many tie-ins including the roof which could be retro fitted with solar panels. Ecological Architect Carrie Bergie suggested a wind turbine atop the 107-foot structure, fiber optic lights and green walls with vertical plant growth which would allow the building to sustain itself.

I wrote editorials, I tried to rally support, but no one really seemed to care. Like many other things in Niagara Falls including the destruction of the Stanford White train station, the Wintergarden was razed in 2008.

# THREE WEDDING DRESSES

In 1985 the Assistant City Manager and Board member Nick M. called me to tell me that the new Earl Brydges Library leaked. The city needed to reclaim the old Carnegie Library space to be used as a library again. Repairs were being made to the new library by the original builder. This was politics as usual.

Nick would help us find another location. I was familiar with the plaza footprint because, for the previous nine years, I had programmed that space every Saturday and Sunday evening during the summer. He moved us to a location that defies description. Suffice as to say it was in the middle of the E. Dent Lackey Plaza. It was a hidden, large cement circular bunker buried under a central fountain that, when operational, which was almost never, sent water shooting upwards toward the sky. Nick was my friend. He ordered circular modules for the staff offices and brought in new office furniture. He carpeted the cold damp walls and, and since there was no natural light, added warm lighting. Unlike most people in the community, he loved and realized the importance the arts and he really tried to help us. There was no room for the deceased Ms. Mossell's concert grand piano so we passed it on to the new Castellani Art Museum at Niagara University.

The direction of the arts council's programming was forced to change without the use of the Carnegie building. Our gallery exhibits hit the road. With portable exhibition walls we moved artworks into several locations.

The Rainbow Mall had recently been built in the of heart of the downtown area of Niagara Falls just two blocks from the Falls and next to the spectacular Wintergarden.

The city proclaimed that the block wide mall would offer a great addition for visitors. I was offered art exhibition space on a sunny second floor level right next to the elevators. It seemed like such a good idea at the time because both local shoppers and tourists could enjoy works by our fine area artists. My colleague, CS, was an art installer who measured each art work hanging in all of our exhibitions to perfection. The mall manager promised us the space, but also told a local exercise group that they could be there too. Three days a week the panels were shoved to the side by overweight women and replaced by exercise mats. Pictures went askew and were out of order. There was no respect for the artists or their work. We had to find another space.

One of my board members had a connection with the Occidental Chemical which was located a block away. Their new downtown building was the first building in North America to be constructed with a Double-Skin Facade. Built after the 1970's oil environmental crisis, the company's new building was touted as the most energy efficient building in the world. The CEO thought that having an art gallery on the main level of this building would be an excellent public relations vehicle. Both the arts council and Oxi-Chem scheduled our annual Juried Western New York Art

Show with great hype. The show was adjudicated by three well respected artists from Buffalo. The selected "Best of Show" turned out to be a painting with a strong environmental and anti-pollution message. Jean, from the company's public relations department, told me that because of the subject matter, the piece could not be hung. My job was to support the artist. We reached a compromise since every year that company gave me a check for $5,000. We hung the winning selection in the back of the lobby in a corner facing an outside wall. I found having to do that very offensive and sad. That show spelled the end of our gallery exhibitions.

***

ArtWheels, our children's art program, was moved to one of the two spaces located in the building arches of the Convention Center, on the upper level of the street facing the Convention Center. This proved to be an adequate and a central city location for our students and patrons. We continued to have four certified art teachers drive two vans with art programs in every county community. We were never charged rent by the city and continued to get an annual grant. I owed it all to my friend Nick. The other arch was occupied by the Niagara Falls Chamber of Commerce who needed a larger and more glamorous space. When they moved out, we moved right in, and finally we could see a hint of daylight again. I hated that underground location.

We organized the first National Very Special Arts Festival with special guest Jean Kennedy Smith. She had a cold attitude and was not at all impressed with the interior of the Convention Center. She asked me if the building was a subway station.

Families and their special children came from all over the United States to participate. We filled a lot of hotel rooms that weekend.

For a number of years on Sunday afternoons in February, the Niagara Council of the Arts presented a popular Poetry series organized by downstate poet Joan Murray. While the north winter wind howled outside, the best of Buffalo area poets read their work in the warmth of this cozy green space. Both the artists and the many listeners felt the venue was perfect.

***

The Niagara Council of the Arts, with its successful Niagara Summer Experience series, was one of only a few summer entertainment venues for tourists on the American side. There wasn't much to do after seeing the Falls themselves. Visitors just took the bridge to Canada without stopping on the American side. The winter months were as dead as my garden. Based on the success of our summer programs, I decided to have an annual Niagara Winter Experience to take place on the first weekend of each February. This could be a vehicle to expand tourism, even if it was only for three days.

I chose that weekend to take advantage of an event that already took place annually, a large and successful hockey tournament, mostly with Canadian teams.

That first year the hockey tournament organizer invited me to lunch to meet their weekend special guest. I was introduced to a quiet young man and his sister. We had a lovely lunch and I said goodbye. When I got home that night I told my three sons about the upcoming hockey tournament and that I had lunch with someone by the name of Wayne Gretzky. They were flabbergasted.

I selected a penguin for the logo of the Niagara Winter Experience and had black and white flags made for all of the lamp posts in the downtown area. This was the perfect tie in with our local Aquarium. I added entertainment, an ice sculpture competition, winter programs in the nearby New York State park, a talent competition for Miss Winter Experience, a pow-wow at the Turtle which was our local Native American Center, and a winter outdoor Boy Scout Camporee. Hundreds of Western New York Scouts erected tents for the weekend and built fires on a vacant city block that was located next to the Convention Center.

I thought it would be a good idea to have food available and make a bit of money at the same time. I found a Niagara County farmer who could bring and cook an ox for an outdoor ox roast. Early on Saturday morning the farmer/cook set up a large drum of charcoals. The beast was skewered from its neck to its derriere and lowered onto the coals with a winch. As the beast rotated on the spit, the two hind legs flopped apart in a most obscene way. I asked the man to tie those two legs together which he found amusing, and by late-afternoon, the ox was done. In Western New York we have a favorite food called Beef on Weck. I had purchased Kimmelweck rolls, bags of potato chips and local horseradish to present Ox on Weck. As the meat was disappearing, Sam drove to a popular local restaurant for pans of regular sliced roast beef and gravy. Patrons kept remarking on how much the ox tasted just like beef. Everyone loved it.

***

The city was in a steep decline. Industry was leaving because of the litigation and environmental repercussions of Love Canal. As a consequence, people were leaving too. The population dived from over a hundred thousand to fifty thousand people. Those interesting and shiny curved wooden seats in the E. Dent Lackey Plaza had deteriorated and those few attending had to sit on old wood that could give you a sliver in the best place. Over the years the brass lips and railings of all of the stairs had been removed at night by vandals with crowbars, then sold for scrap. All of the wiring attached to the lights under the plaza railings had been pulled out and vandalized. The welcoming bright red carpeting in the underground tunnel was now dirty and stained with urine. It was a glorious run for all of these Arts Council's presentations but something had changed. When we began using the downtown space, thousands would attend. On some nights I had to call for traffic control. When we ended the program twenty-two years later, the number of people attending was down to about 200 each night. People would tell me that they didn't want to park downtown because they felt that it was dirty, rundown and it wasn't safe.

One of my suburban friends said, "why would I take my wife to that dirty downtown when I can go to so many other places"?

There was never a spare minute. On the home front the three girls and I loved our small house in the village. I planted a very large raised vegetable garden, all neatly separated by plants and railroad ties provided by Sam. My bay window was filled with three glass shelves of African Violets from Frances.

Mary Helen was in high school and so I attended her many school violin concerts and art shows. In 1984 I found time to make Joan her wedding dress, a satin off-the-shoulder design. She wore a crown of fresh flowers in her hair, and she was just as beautiful as her soul continues to be. We all laughed when we she walked down the aisle with a needle and thread dangling from the back of her dress.

When I look back at those years, I had boundless energy. I never missed a day of work. I continued to fly back and forth to New York City on State business. I always took the earliest flight, took a cab from the airport to the NYSCA office in lower Manhattan, left by 4:30 p.m. to ride back to the airport to catch the last plane back to Buffalo. Landing during the winter months was always dicey. I often flew to some other far away art organization or conference to be a consultant, speaker or a panelist.

I could not foresee my personal life changing so I decided that I should seek a new job. I got down to the final three candidates in a national search for the position of Executive Director of the King County Art Commission in Seattle. The county had instituted a 1% tax on all new construction which would then be used for public art. I loved the concept, but they hired from within.

I also was a finalist when applying for the job of Executive Director of the Texas Arts Commission. I flew to Austin and took a cab to the hotel that they had selected for me. It was the historic Driskill Hotel, Lyndon B. Johnsons favorite hotel. It wasn't so strange that all of Austin's Hospitality was directed to that hotel.

The window of my room faced a brick wall, not a great thought if there was an emergency. I was tired from my flight and turned down the spread only to find a foot round hole in the middle of the blanket. I called the front desk and asked for another room. I was told that that was given to me because it was the least expensive room in the hotel. I paid the difference for an upgrade. The next day, as per my instructions, I took a cab to a tall downtown building that was totally empty because it was a Saturday. My instructions said to go to a room number on the fifth floor. There was no one to meet me, so I entered a very large open room with about a dozen desks. It was very quiet except for the drone of the overhead fluorescent lights. I heard the elevator door open and a man came into the room with a list of questions for me to answer in two hours. He gave me a handful of sharpened #2 pencils and said he would be back.

I stalled when the test included a very complicated and unexpected math question. Remember no cell phones back then. I just couldn't figure out how to solve the math problem and the next thing I knew, I heard the elevator door open and the man was back again. He took me to another floor that had a Board room. I was not prepared for the stogy all male hiring committee's questions about Texas artists. I failed miserably. I resorted to my favorite adage which says that everything happens for a reason.

Back in Niagara Falls my family, arts management, fundraising, presentations and positive interfacing with community groups continued to eat away the hours. Many weekends were devoted to business somewhere in the State, and then there was the Road Scholar programs that were so successful that they became a job unto themselves.

***

Of course, since I made a wedding dress for one daughter, I had to make each of the other two sisters their dresses too. Judy was next to get married in 1990. Her dress was made of a beautiful lace and sequin material, so reflective of Judy because she continues to sparkle in all that she does.

Two years later Mary Helen, my artistic one, sketched out a pattern for a satin dress with leg of mutton sleeves. I added 1,000 seed pearls, graduated in size, from shoulder to wrist on each of the sleeves. The dress was pure Mary Helen in its brilliant design and creativity. For the next five years I found those damnable loose pearls under and in all of the furniture and rugs.

# ANOTHER JIM

As my career as the Executive Director continued in the mid 80's I was often asked to speak at or attend Niagara County community functions, especially in Niagara Falls. My 'friend' Sam was invited to many of the same functions in our business community and I always sat with him and his wife as a kind of third wheel. I hated that arrangement. Under these circumstances and after an intimate relationship with him of eleven years, I felt uncomfortable, deceitful, and discontented. Plus, I liked her. She was always so good to my daughter Joan, giving her a bridal shower and constantly pouring love from her generous heart.

In January of 1985 the annual Chamber of Commerce dinner was held in the largest ballroom in Niagara Falls. I found myself as a third wheel once again. While we were inside, a heavy winter snowstorm had moved in over the lake. When the event was over all of the gentlemen went down into the snow-filled parking lot to brush and retrieve their buried car, then pick up their partner from under the portico. There was no one but me to act like one of the boys, plodding through the snow with my flimsy sexy sandals, my hair blowing in the wind. Then and there I made up my mind. I would not attend any more functions unless I had an escort. No more third wheel. I'd rather stay home.

In February the Cristoforo Columbus Society had their annual dinner dance. I knew I should go because that organization always assisted me with the summer Italian Festival. I told Sam that I would not be going unless I had a date. He reminded me that there was a recently divorced gentleman from Buffalo who was working in the Italian section of the city, and perhaps he would take me. I realized that I had recently denied this same individual a grant for his business district, so he probably would not be interested. I was surprised when he called me, asked me to go to the dinner and got my address to pick me up. No physical moves on his part. He was a real gentleman and his name was Jim Lodico.

Another Jim, but this one was so much different from the Irish father of my children. The Jim who phoned me was from the west side of Buffalo, home to many second-generation Italian families. He had had a career in Retail Management, a job that required good judgment and people skills. His career included managing a series of Hens and Kelly Department stores, one of the higher end department stores in Western New York. Hens and Kelly's, like so many other department stores, closed its doors, and Jim was out of a job. At one time he had three hundred women working under his supervision. He was divorced, had five children who, after his divorce, had hung him out to dry thanks to his negative and demeaning wife. They did not respect him in the least. The series of unfortunate events including his recent unemployment and his divorce, took a physical and mental toll on him. He was poorer than a church mouse.

Our courtship was unusual. For the first few months, we would occasionally meet after work at about 5 p.m. at the same local watering hole. He was pleasant, interesting, and he paid for each of our single drinks, usually a Manhattan. I was surprised to learn that he loved classical music, especially music by Tomaso Albinoni, the Italian Baroque composer. He enjoyed art galleries and he yearned to travel. He was a practicing Catholic, tipped his hat when passing a church and always carried a rosary. He never pushed himself on me, and he never showed any inclination to hold my hand or give me a brief kiss good-bye. We talked about our days activities then he would go his way and I would go mine.

Mine was to drive to Buffalo to meet Francis for supper or to take him for his anti-distress drive. I'd be home by 8:30 p.m. Many times, he would stop at my house to watch the 11:00 p.m. news. My three daughters were getting on with their lives. Judy had graduated from nursing school at Niagara University, Joan was a new mother and Mary Helen planned to go to art school in Buffalo.

Given the situation between Sam and ME, Sam thought it was a great joke that he was playing on Jim Lodico regarding our initial date. After his divorce, Jim had moved to Niagara Falls to begin his job as Marketing Manager of the Pine Avenue Business Association. That organization promoted the fact that Pine Avenue catered to anything Italian. The area included a mother church and many Italian restaurants. The business group anticipated that tourists to the area would shop at their properties. Sam was active in that same organization and offered Jim a place to stay in a room over his office. After a short period of time Jim was smart enough to realize that Sam expected favors in return for his hospitality and decided it would be wise to move to a space owned by his friend and former shoe salesman George Corsaro.

After a few months, he called me and asked me to go on an actual date. He suggested dinner in Niagara Falls, Canada, at a spaghetti joint called Mama Mia's. He was charming, witty, polite and interesting during the meal. He was surprised and embarrassed that he didn't have enough money to pay the bill, so we laughed and split the tab. We laughed a lot together which was part of my attraction to him.

I had one reservation about a permanent relationship between us. Was he as cold as Jim Allen or was he reticent to begin a physical relationship? Given a little more time, a few months in fact, he answered my question by inviting me to come and see his "place".

His "place" was a single room and kitchenette in a not-so-great neighbourhood. He slept in a borrowed cot and his clothes were neatly distributed in three cardboard boxes along the wall. Dishes were piled in the sink. I was aghast.

***

I found myself having very deep feelings for him. We were sympatico, and it seemed that we were spending more and more time together. I invited Jim to move into our little house in Lewiston. He said yes, which really turned out to mean "let the adventures together begin".

It was time for me to burn my bridges to the past. I asked Sam to meet me in the State park where we often had lunch together. He was not prepared to hear that Jim and I were planning to live together. I ended that long-time relationship. That same week I met Francis to tell him about Jim. He understood the fact that I was young enough to want a meaningful and permanent loving partner. Both Jim Allen and Jim Lodico knew about Sam, but neither knew about Francis.

Late that summer I thought it would be nice to have a picnic in our yard and my family could meet Jim's family. Once, he had shared the fact that his sister Kathy was a little person, but I wasn't prepared to actually see this wonderful and unusual family. The picnic was to begin at four o'clock.

Right at the appointed time a little "Sunbeam" auto pulled up in front of the house. I watched from behind the curtain. Out came his sister Kathy, her husband, and two sons. All were little people. The doorbell was too high, so Kathy rang the bell with the end of her cane. They tumbled in just as his sister Alberta "Bertie" pulled up in a van, the outside of which was painted with a hippie pink and mauve mountain scene. Her husband Tim towered over her.

His sister Bertie was a revelation. Dressed in a tight sweater, this buxom sister wore such tight jeans that some kind of lubricant must have been used to pull those pants into position. Her short frame stood on high wooden platform heels. Her black hair was teased high on the top of her head and her eyes were painted like Nefertiti. The other half of the couple, Jim's brother-in-law Tim, took my breath away. He could have been a poster boy for "Hell's Angels". He was an imposing six foot four figure with shoulder length greying curly hair, navy blue denim jeans and jacket with the appropriate silver key chain draped from his pocket, all topped off with leather wrist bands and motorcycle boots. My girls were just starting to process Jim's sister Kathy's little family when Bertie and Tim walked into the yard. They gasped.

I've said enough about my unusual and unforgettable first meeting with Jim's family. Over 34 years they have become very special in my life.

***

Jim Lodico's high school friend Joseph Pillittere had become a New York State Assemblyman representing Niagara Falls and environs. He asked Jim to come and work for him as an Administrative Assistant. His new office was on Pine Avenue, in the heart of the Italian district.

***

After a couple of years our Lewiston nest was empty so I sold the house and Jim and I moved to rent a beautiful apartment in the historic Red Coach Inn just across the street from the Niagara River and the State park. The Falls were just a half block away.

We were both abundantly happy and content, so much so that after a year and a half, Jim decided that we could finally get married.

On May 22, 1987, the Niagara Falls Convention and Visitors Bureau held their seasonal kick-off breakfast at "the Turtle" located next door to our apartment. Because of our jobs, both Jim and I attended the breakfast. When the event was over our friend Mayor Michael O'Laughlin joined a small group gathered next to the river. He pronounced us man and wife. In attendance were

Jim's mother Rose and his four children, two of my daughters, (Judy was in California), his best friend Pete Montane and my best friend Jan Montazzolli who were our witnesses.

The following day was a Saturday, and I had scheduled a Road Scholar trip for the Niagara Council of the Arts months in advance. Early that morning my new husband Jim and I made and packed forty-eight lunches for the bus trip to Stratford, Ontario, Canada but we added champagne and a wedding cake for a surprise announcement of our wedding. How many people can say that they had their wedding reception on a bus in a foreign country? It was a short but memorable celebration. There were many adventures to follow. Jim just went along with all of my unusual requests with curiosity and cheer.

One of the more outrageous requests I made of my new husband Jim took place in the State park across the street from the Red Coach where we lived. I asked him to help me bury my friend.

Years before, I had met a woman by the name of Irene when she came to my office and asked to be a volunteer for the Niagara Council of the Arts. Because she was alone, she became like a member of my family and joined my family on special holidays. I found it hard to believe that this five foot, rather ordinary looking woman claimed to be a Hungarian Countess. But then again, she could speak eight languages and had the knowledge and manners of a very cultured person. I met her sister who was visiting from Switzerland and she had the title of Baroness. As the years went on, she told me about many of her European wartime experiences.

She told me that when the Germans stormed into her family's villa in 1944, the soldiers smashed all of the Czechoslovakian cut crystal in the vitrines that lined the family's huge dining room walls. Her family fled by train to Vienna carrying a number of suitcases. In one was a pair of 15 inch Hungarian dolls dressed in traditional costumes, a boy and a girl, their faces made out of wax. It was so hot on the train that the eyes of one of the dolls melted shut. She gave me those dolls, one year at a time, telling me how much they meant to her. I have given them to my granddaughter Katie to treasure because of her Hungarian heritage.

I believe that she was a Jew, although she never told me that. Her travel west towards America was dangerous and included her going underground in France under the guidance and assistance of the 'Maquis'. Along the way she shared a train compartment through France to London with a woman who was carrying a hatbox with a false compartment fitted with her jewels. She gave Irene her family address in the UK just in case the Gestapo caught her. Sure enough, the train made an impromptu stop, and soldiers boarded the train. Irene was petrified since she was wanted too. They took the other woman away. Irene took possession of the box and days later delivered the contents to the address written on the note. There were many twists and turns in her journey, and she ended up pretty much alone in a shabby second floor flat in downtown Niagara Falls. She died of pneumonia and since there was no money to bury her, I talked a local funeral director into cremating her as an act of charity. He gave me her ashes in a small nondescript cardboard box and I kept them on my desk. A year later they were still sitting there.

Very early on a glorious sunny May morning, I said to Jim, “Get up, we’re going to bury Irene this morning”.

I drove to my office to pick up the cardboard box from my desk, then drove back to our apartment to pick up Jim. We then drove onto the bridge leading us to Goat Island and there, ahead of us, was an apple tree in full bloom, its snow-white petals glistening from a combination of the mist of the Falls and the very early morning sun. He pulled the car over in silence. We laid her to rest in this place of forever peace and everlasting beauty. Good night Irene.

# THE FBI

I have had an interesting and close relationship with stockings my whole life. In the beginning, I had to deal with those ugly thick black wool stockings worn with bloomers, a part of the St. Joseph's College School uniform. They were very hot and itchy in the warmer weather and were held up by a circular cotton garter belt, the kind with four appendages hanging downwards from below the waist. Today, the same apparatus produced in sheer lace is considered sexy and hot in a different way.

I was too young to wear nylons during World War II. That was the era of the nylon stocking with the seam down the back. Just as well that I missed that time period because, knowing me, my seam would always have been crooked. As I got older, I fairly swooned at the lucky women in the stocking department who would pick out a flat box from an endless pile, open the box and the soft tissue paper, make a fist, pull the top of the enclosed stocking over that fist, revealing to the client how the color would look on her leg. It never took much to make me happy. And then someone, somewhere, invented pantyhose.

In 1976 my son Tom played the lead part in the Niagara Falls High School musical "Jesus Christ Super Star". That day, I had an early morning meeting and for the rest of the day the work rhythm was totally exhausting. At closing time, I went home, cooked dinner for eight, and since the whole family planned to attend the play that night, I went upstairs, took my slacks off and fell sound asleep on the bed. Someone woke me up and told me to hurry. I grabbed a pair of panty hose from my drawer, pulled my slacks back on top, and off we all went to high school.

We paid our admission, bought the obligatory nasty orange drink and proceeded down the long hall lined with brown metal lockers to the auditorium.

Somebody in the family pointed and said "what's that?"

I look down behind me and a nylon foot was protruding from each pant leg opening and dragging on the ground. Now more theatre goers were looking at the bottom of my pants as I proceeded forward down the hall. More, longer pantyhose legs appeared from each of the leg holes of my slacks.

I got to my seat and started yanking to extract the extra pair of hose. It seems that when I went for my nap, I had left the first pair of hose inside of my slacks. I had added a second pair in my haste.

***

In 1985 I had another stocking embarrassment. That was the year that the Niagara Reservation of the New York State Park system celebrated the 100th year anniversary as the oldest State park in the nation. The park was just across the street from where Jim and I lived. In its wisdom the State decided that they wanted a celebration that would be a tourism multiplier. A VIP committee of prestigious Western New Yorkers was put together in July of the previous year, chaired by KB an overbearing socialite from along the river in Lewiston. She, in turn, wanted me to plan and organize a particular week-end of events. She called me at the Arts Council to set up a meeting and discuss content and payment. We had never met.

"I'd like to meet you for lunch, but the 'club' is closed on Wednesdays." she said with haughty dry voice. "Do you know where the Niagara Club is?"

I answered "yes", not explaining that I lived next door.

"Fine, I'll meet you on Wednesday at one".

I remember I had such an appetite that day. I looked forward to a hefty sandwich and a glass of white wine. I was already seated when Mrs. B. came in. She appeared unhealthy, pale and as thin as a rake. Her collar bones appeared to be two handles set below her neck. She ordered Perrier, and I said that I would have the same. She ordered steamed vegetables and I again made the order for two. I had many questions for her.

In all of my business dealings I always made it a point to give the other person my full attention by looking them right in the eye. The steamed vegetables were served still steaming. I have a very sensitive nose and the steam made my nose drip. I reached down into my purse which was on the floor beside me. I didn't look down, I just continued to listen to Mrs. B. Suddenly I realized that I was wiping my nose with the toe of a hanging half pantyhose leg. I was so surprised and gave her a weak smile, not interrupting my gaze. She grimaced in her astonishment. I had taken my daughter Mary Helen for school shoes the day before and had chopped off a piece of hose for her shoe shopping. It was no wonder that I was never invited to any of her exclusive committee parties.

It was made clear to me that my sole job was to program the park during the two day event. Everything else would be looked after by a committee member, including traffic control and publicity. I made suggestions about possible parking issues, but I was told not to worry.

I set up two stages at opposite ends of the park. Both locations had scheduled ongoing events. I worked with the Niagara Frontier Folk Arts Society in Buffalo to program colorful performances. The Buffalo Philharmonic would play. I hired two harpists to play at the waters' edge and strolling musicians to interface with the visitors. I did my part to make the event memorable.

In the weeks ahead of the event, I kept watching TV and the Buffalo and Niagara Falls newspapers for the publicity generated by the highly rated Buffalo firm that Mrs. B. had hired. There was none. A couple of weeks before the celebration I called Madame Chairman but she said that I should not worry, it would be done. But it wasn't. Jim and I sat in a golf cart and waited for the crowds. The entertainers waited for an audience. With no publicity, the event was a total disaster.

***

Because I had been so active in promoting and producing tourism events in the downtown area of Niagara Falls, I was asked to be a member of the Niagara County Tourism Advisory Board.

Monthly meetings were held in the evenings at Niagara County Community College in the middle of the county. The drive was beautiful for the spring and fall but in winter I faithfully drove alone across windswept, dark and snowy county road to attend. It was an effort, but I took this honour seriously. At my first meeting I was immediately disillusioned because the Niagara County Tourism chairman, whom I'll call Tony G., would enter each meeting after having already met before the meeting with his chosen buddies to decide major issues. We other committee members were only there as "yes" men.

Tony G. owned a number of information stands outside of Niagara Falls where his employees would steer tourists to his chosen hotels and restaurants for a kick-back. He also sold tours using his fleet of tour buses. He owned the bus company, the Parkway Ramada Hotel, a motel, restaurant, tourism booths on every major entrance into the city and it was said that he controlled 500 hotel rooms in the Falls. Signage to Niagara Falls in all directions took visitors the long way to the downtown area. Rather than put up correct signage, he declared that it was better for tourists to get lost looking for Niagara Falls than to have clear directions that might lead them to Canada. In 1986 there was a series of tourism booth bombings in Niagara County. Two of Tony's rivals' booths were bombed, and an unexploded gasoline bomb was found near one of Tony's. No charges were ever placed. The following year, a team from the FBI, IRS, and the State Police seized thousands of documents from Tony's businesses, but again no charges were pressed.

***

One evening in 1989 Jim and I had an interesting conversation over dinner. He told me that there was a new businessman in town that he was working with. Jim thought he was a neat guy, planned to play golf with him and he would try to assist him in any way. The man had plans to start a 40 million dollar honeymoon development in the Falls. He wanted to secure space in the State Park to put in concessions, which is against the law. Jim told him that this was illegal but perhaps they could locate somewhere else. The man's name was Dennis Tirro. Jim would help him secure an office for Tirro Enterprises on the third floor of his building, right above the New York State Assembly office. All of a sudden Dennis was seen everywhere in town, joining the every Wednesday noon lunch group at the Como, a popular Italian restaurant and picking up the tab at the Municipal golf course for many new friends. He even handed me a one hundred dollar bill for a membership in the Arts Council at some event that we both attended. He only dealt in cash. He was very personable, and he wangled his way into every party or gathering.

Jim was becoming one of his best friends. Jim was a fan of the Buffalo Bills, but I was not really interested. One day he came home to ask me if I would go with him to attend a game with Dennis and some other acquaintances. Dennis had a brand new RV which would be filled with food from that Italian Restaurant and plenty of booze. I said yes to make Jim happy. On the game day the RV pulled up in front of the Red Coach where we joined the Mayor and his wife Donna, Assemblyman Joe Pillittere and his wife Joan, the popular County Coroner Jimmy Joyce and his wife, and Dennis and his girlfriend who looked taller and older than him. They just didn't match. We set out for The Ralph

Wilson Stadium which was 30 miles away. Dennis said, no worries, he had hired a driver for the day. We were immediately offered generous drinks, with quick refills. After the game hundreds of cars left the parking lots, but Dennis said we should just stay for a while, let the crowds pass and, of course, have something to eat and another drink. We finally left the parking lot to head home, but a very short distance away the driver moved the RV over to a silver guardrail on the side of the highway and announced that there was something wrong with the RV's electrical system. We would have to wait for someone to come and rescue us. We later found out that a car had been following us with FBI agents and sound equipment. The highway noise was distorting our conversations in the RV ahead. They sent a message to the driver to pull over and have us wait. Time to have another drink. After about thirty minutes a fifteen-seat van pulled up in front of us. The driver? Tony G., former Niagara County Tourism Director and bomber, who had made a deal to act as Dennis Tirro's business partner. He was now working for the FBI. I found out some time later that the FBI has a video of Jim and me now on file in Washington. Dennis and his girlfriend turned out to be undercover FBI agents. He had bugged Jim's office just below Tirro Enterprises. For eighteen months he was looking for crooked politicians and businessmen in Niagara Falls. The Buffalo Bills tickets, the RV and driver, the food and drinks were compliments of the FBI. The idea behind the trip was a sting to loosen tongues with that demon rum, and hope someone would say something to incriminate themselves or others.

***

The Arts Council Road Scholar program was very successful. Over the years I hired dozens of buses. If the bus company was American, most of the time the drivers worked part time on the weekend and didn't have much pride in their work, including sloppy attire. The Canadian bus company drivers were always very professional, always fitted with a smart uniform and a smile. Each Canadian driver was fussy about the cleanliness of his bus. Because of the exchange rate, and because of the drivers and their buses, I began just using Canadian buses. The Canadian drivers got to know me, and because they knew that they would get a generous tip at the end of the day, they tried to get my assignment. For many months I was sent the same red headed driver Joe, who lived with his wife and young daughter in Fort Erie, Ontario.

We traveled to the theatre in Toronto almost every Saturday, and as time went on Joe became more comfortable and more familiar with us. He was always so unusually happy. If Jim and I had seen the production we would just stay in the bus, and Joe would leave us for a couple of hours, roller skates draped around his neck. The true fact was that he was going to roll with a Toronto sweetie.

One Saturday the company sent another driver.

I said, "Where's Joe?"

The new driver said, "His wife found him dead in their garage. He committed suicide."

It seems that Joe was having a serious relationship with a Japanese woman in Toronto. His guilt overtook him.

***

Once, after a particular long Saturday Road Scholar trip Toronto, our Canadian bus crossed over the Rainbow bridge to disembark people five blocks away at the Convention Center. There, drivers would be waiting to bring the theatre goers home.

Usually when we return to the United States and the bus is full of over forty-nine sleepy gray hairs, an officer would come on board, take a cursory look at ID's and send the bus on its way. Not this time. Instead, the bus was ordered to pull over and all forty-seven people were told to get out and enter the building. There is something about crossing the border, talking to a man in uniform, and waiting. Some people were afraid. There weren't any cell phones yet, with no communication with those waiting at the Convention Center.

Jim took the officer aside and gave him his card which indicated that he worked for New York State. No one there would give us a reason for this delay. Finally, after many phone calls, the driver was told that he could not bring the bus into the USA. He would have to leave the riders in that waiting room and go back to Canada. Jim and I, plus two officers, boarded and emptied the bus before it turned around.

Jim asked the officer if he would drive him to the Convention Center to pick up our ArtWheels van. He made several trips back and forth to bring the stranded travelers to their waiting rides.

I wanted and needed an answer as to what was going on. Remember Niagara County Tourism chairman, Tony G. and the FBI. He owned an American bus company and it seems he was upset with me because I was using a Canadian company and not his. He convinced local officials that since I receive money from New York State agencies, I should not be allowed to take my bus business to Canada. I would be made an example to not use Canadian buses. There was nothing that I could do. After about a year, I went back to Canadian buses.

# BLANCHE, A NEW AMERICAN CITIZEN

On the other side of the country, my mother Blanche loved her California lifestyle. My brother Paul was living on his own. During her first years in Santa Monica she met John, a Captain with American Airlines, and for many years they dated, spent time together and went to the best restaurants. One day he surprised her by informing her that he had found a much younger companion. Her vanity wounded, she had married a man younger than herself, a handsome German gentleman by the name of Ray Moesinger. Originally from Iowa, he was injured in the Second World War and suffered serious injury to both of his legs. Shortly after her marriage to him, he was sent to the Veterans Hospital in Oregon for surgery where he remained for a number of years.

Blanche kept busy working at the Santa Monica Beach Club and with the actress June Lockhart. At that same time she took care of her baby sister Helena who was terminally ill with cancer.

After a number of years Ray returned to Santa Monica where he made my mother's life generally miserable. He took over her long-established routine of living, including her joy of listening to classical music. He constantly demeaned her and had a twenty-four hour nasty and mean disposition. It was mental cruelty. Shortly after I married Jim Lodico, we flew to California so that he could meet my mother. As soon as we arrived Ray disappeared and returned back just in time for us to treat for dinner. It was only a short walk to the restaurant in Beverly Hills called Hamburger Hamlet. I selected this place because, silly me, that it sounded less expensive than the rest of the restaurants in her neighbourhood. As soon as I saw the doorman, I knew that I had been wrong. I had made a reservation, and before dinner we ordered a drink in the large crowded bar area. My mother ordered Whiskey Sour that immediately angered Ray because, in his judgment, no one in their right mind would do that. That set the tone. After a long wait, our table was finally ready. When we arrived at our table my mother would not sit down because she felt that because she had a French accent she was made to sit next to the kitchen entrance, which was farthest from the truth. The hostess just smiled and took us back to the bar side for another long wait. We finally were ushered into another dining room, ordered and ate our meal in silence, after which Jim went to use the men's room. While he was gone, my mother asked the waitress for a "dogee bag". That set Ray off again, telling my mother and the surrounding tables that we can afford food, and we didn't need a "dogee bag".

I said, "Ray, people do this all of the time". I think he had watched one too many World War II German movies. He slowly got up from his chair and placed both hands on the table. He drew himself up to his full Germanic stature, and with a look of pure distain said loud enough for all to hear, "You're nothing but a piece of shit". I think I heard his heels click under the table. He placed a wooden tooth pick between his lips before storming off in a huff. We never saw him again during our visit.

He just disappeared. It took a while for me to convince Jim that we should go back to California to visit my mother again. In

1993 we arrived at her apartment and she was crying. She told us that Ray was in bed and that his legs were black. One look under his sheets convinced us that he needed to get to the hospital immediately. We ordered an ambulance and followed him in a cab to the Veterans Hospital in Los Angeles. He never came home and died shortly after.

It seemed like the right time to have my mother come and live closer to us. We were able to rent her an apartment at The Red Coach just above our apartment but after a year she needed more care. She was eighty-seven years old when she moved thirty minutes away from me to Lockport, NY to a wonderful "skilled facility". The Social Worker called me many times to tell me that she wouldn't socialize or participate in any of the activities, including playing cards. She really believed that her years in Brentwood made her better than 'all of doz stoopid people". At her 90th birthday party, attended by many my children and her great grandchildren, she looked and acted like Norma Desmond in Sunset Boulevard. Nothing indicated her difficult early years. A year later she fell, and Briarwood would no longer keep her there. My daughter Judy researched and did all of the complicated job of obtaining SSI for my mother. This Social Security program supplemented and assisted people with limited income, but also prohibited her from living in one of the better nursing homes. A social worker told us that because she was not an American citizen, her SSI might be taken away.

There was only one thing to do. We had to get her to swear allegiance to the American flag as soon as possible. I made an appointment for her to appear for an initial inquiry regarding citizenship in downtown Buffalo.

The day of her appointment she said that she didn't want to go, so I went alone with the excuse that she was ill. I entered a large room lined with benches. Every seat was taken and everyone looked weary. They looked like they had been waiting a long time.

I went to the office window and said to the secretary, "I'm here representing Mrs. Moesinger".

I looked very professional in my black wool suit, black suede opera pumps and my obligatory strand of pearls. I carried my large black leather briefcase.

The secretary said, "please come right in" and to my surprise, she buzzed me into the next room.

I immediately realized that she thought that I was Mrs. Moesinger's attorney. I didn't tell her otherwise. I explained that Mrs. Moesinger was very sick and had one dying wish. She wanted to die an American citizen, which was the farthest thing from the truth. Patriotism is a complicated feeling and Blanche never knew that kind of love. I embellished.

The secretary and her co-workers became emotional. She set up an appointment for an official to go to the nursing home the next week. She herself would do the necessary paperwork.

Blanche was 91 years old when, holding a small American flag for effect, she became an American citizen. She died in my arms at age 93. Her ashes are buried beside my father Jack in Thornhill, Ontario.

***

When the calendar turned to January of 1999 I was feeling exceedingly burned out, mostly in the politics department. I was tired at being nice to everyone while secretly I believed that I was dealing with mostly mindless people with huge egos. I knew it was time to retire. I set the date at Jan 2, 2000.

In July I began to prepare. I made sure that all of the files and public relations gleaned over twenty-five years were in order. I painted and freshened my office space, guided a Search Committee through a hiring process but I stayed out of any decision making. Everything was in order, including a bit of money in the bank and the Pavarotti account. The committee interviewed the finalist and hired a woman from Buffalo.

***

Autumn delivered some crisp air and a surprising letter. It was from the Executive Director of the Alliance of New York State Arts Councils who wrote me that I would receive the first award for Advancing Community Arts Development for New York State. The award would be given to me at Lincoln Center in New York City in 1999 and would thereafter be called the M. Jacquie Lodico Award for Distinguished Service.

In early December, over fifty of my art associates from Western New York flew to the Big Apple to support and join me in accepting this wonderful honour. I did not have an acceptance speech prepared ahead of time, but when I mounted the dais, the words just poured out. My three daughters, my eldest son Tim and my husband Jim joined in the celebration. Never in my wildest dreams did I think that I would stand on a stage in Lincoln Center.

***

I started the new century feeling free as a bird and happy as a clam as I contemplated my retirement. No more 7:30 a.m. breakfast meetings on the other side of the county and no more worrying about income and cash flow. It would be just Jim and me.

I met with the new arts council Executive Director before she started in her new position. She wanted no part of the Road Scholar travel program, a facet of the arts council that was important to many people and supported the earned income side of the budget. I offered to keep the program going. Jim and I would get a free trip and I would give any income generated back to the arts council. She said no. I told her that I would give her six months in case she changed her mind, but she didn't.

***

February 2000 was my month for accepting awards. Early in February 800 people attended the Chamber of Commerce dinner and gave special recognition to my community accomplishments. In mid-February the Niagara Falls Convention and Visitors Bureau awarded me the 2000 Chairman's Award.

The Chamber had a special glass award made for the occasion. They had installed it next to the dais on a tall stand covered in black velvet. It had a picture of the Falls etched into the front and it was back-lit by a light placed in the back of the tribute. After the dinner, the Master of Ceremony called me to go to the front. After some generous comments he grabbed the glass award by the top and placed it into by outstretched hands. People in the audience were standing and clapping, while my hands were on fire. After such a long period of time, the light had heated the glass to such a temperature that even the four glass tabs on the bottom had melted. I couldn't just throw it. I searched for somewhere to lay it while my palms were burning but I continued to smile. I laid it on the floor to cool.

Later that month, my former board members joined 51 others to honour me with a meaningful retirement party. I especially remember two things. Everyone was seated and just before the meal was served a very tall and handsome African-American gentleman rose from his chair. He beckoned me over. He presented me with the most beautiful two dozen long-stemmed yellow roses and in a weeping voice thanked me and declared to those in attendance that I had made a very big difference in his being. I tearfully accepted his floral tribute. To this day I am not aware of why or how I impacted his life.

It was the perfect time to pass the halo. I took that opportunity to go from table to table, pausing behind each chair for a couple of minutes to thank each attendee and share with those attending why they were so special in my life. Without everyone in that room I would not have achieved some degree of success in my quest to broaden Niagara's cultural horizon.

# THIBERY TOURS, LLC

When we lived at the Red Coach Inn, two dozen eclectic Canadian friends joined each other on Friday nights to listen to music, share stories, and to tipple. Canadians love to party. After twenty-five years, those friends now meet once a month, usually in Canada, each time changing the location. The group has become a support system for one another and has endured through marriages and divorces, sickness and death.

One single gentleman named Terry was my mystery man of the group. The word was that he was a bachelor who had been in the Canadian Navy for many years and had visited many parts of the world. He was a voracious reader and could take part in any conversation no matter what the subject. Each week he would bring me the travel section of the Toronto Star and the New York Times. I filed them in my office for later reference and ideas.

After six months in retirement, I filed the necessary paperwork for my own LLC. which I called Thibery Tours, LLC. I need to tell you why we named our company Thibery.

Just before we were married, I found an ad for an overseas rental apartment in the Toronto Star. A few months later we were off across the ocean and settled in this tiny village seldom found on a map. Thibery (population 1,874) is a small village in the south of France where Jim and I attempted to buy a vacation home some years ago. The property that was for sale was a part of a Benedictine Abbey sitting in the very heart of the tiny town. It was founded in the late 8$^{th}$ century. We gave a real estate agent a deposit but the mayor had to approve the sale. He did not give his approval because he had other plans for the Abbey. When I saw the movie "Chocolat", (available on Amazon Prime) it was like a flash back. The mistral winds, the mayor and the village itself, looked all too familiar.

The old Roman road "Via Domitia" runs through the village (Grand Rue) and past houses dating back to the 15th century. The very narrow road, only a chariot wide, continues on past a wheat mill (*moulin à bled*) which was built in the 13th century and is one of the best preserved mills in the region. Roman graffiti is etched into the back wall.

If you continue on, you can find an ancient Roman bridge which had nine arches, three of which are now missing. These are known to have been destroyed by a flood some time before 1536. The road on the bridge has clearly identifiable ruts made by traveling Roman chariots. The structure is dated to the reign of emperor Augustus (30 BC–14 AD). At the other end of the bridge you are forced to halt and become lost in endless rows of grapevines.

The Roman Saint Thibery, was riding his horse back in Roman times on the Via Domitia passing through this small village, when he was thrown off of his horse. He had a holy apparition and converted to the new Christian faith.

We fell in love with the color, charm, history and the people of this small village and returned many times. Once we attended the village's annual bingo game. I'm not fond of the game but one of our British neighbours said that we really had to go for the experience.

I can safely say that everyone in the village attended, from babes swaddled in a blanket to older residents being pushed in wheelchairs. The back section of the town hall was full of prizes. No money. Instead a quantity of local products such as oysters, shrimp, clams, cheeses, a wide variety of local wines, piglets, many varieties of sausage, honey, jams and fruit.

The Maire (Mayor) sat on a chair in the middle of the stage. On his lap he had a long, narrow royal blue velvet bag that held all of the bingo numbers. Each time he shook the bag and pulled a number, he recited a poem that rhymed with the pulled number. The short poems were about the village and those who lived in it. People hooted and clapped. When someone yelled Bingo, the prize was one of the local food products, then more hooting and clapping. When a young teenage boy got a full card, he need help to carry his loot home. His family invited Jim and me to their village home to share, eat and drink their winnings. What a delightful local experience.

***

I probably could write a tome about travel that I have taken either by myself, with my husband or with a group. Whichever way, it was always an adventure. Adventures don't come easily. You have to be a willing participant, cautious but not overly, and love maps. Being a reader is a must.

Both the Road Scholar program and Thibery Tours LLC allowed my husband and I to take out-of-the-ordinary European trips. I spent many hours selecting the route, the hotels and the menus including the wines.

The first thing I had to decide was what country we were going to explore next. I would select just one country, and usually only a section of that country, at a time. Next, I investigated, both by reading and by Googling, what unique events would be taking place in that area. The event very often shifted my departure date and my route. The trips were usually fourteen days long, and always included lots of free time. I tried not to have the bus leave in the early morning before my fellow travelers had a hearty and sometimes memorable breakfast. The Ritz in Madrid, Spain, and The Penz in Innsbruck, Austria, immediately come to mind. Not many of the selected hotels offered just an orange juice, a hard roll and a cup of coffee.

This reminds me of the disagreeable breakfast and waiter at the Hotel de Palma in Palermo, Sicily. He shook his fists and loudly scolded the young busboy, and when I asked for more coffee, practically threw a cup at me. I selected all of the included dinner menus and wines before we left. I put together a spiral bound book for each traveler. It contained the itinerary, maps and pertinent information about the hotels and places that we would be visiting.

The maximum group was twenty-five people, each of whom had their own unique personality. Many people returned time after time, so as a Tour Director, I often knew what to expect. But not always. It was always an adventure.

Over thirty five years of traveling I dealt with stolen purses, pickpockets, gypsies, lost bags in the airport and in the hotel, heart problems, stomach problems, falls resulting in broken teeth, and broken bones, a fist fight in Greece, lost passports, lost and confused older ladies, not enough rooms available although they were booked months before, a bus in a ditch, a driver who became very ill and couldn't continue, a driver who couldn't speak English, a French driver who had a two week affair with one of the ladies in our group, missed flights, and that is only a start. Each of the items mentioned deserve a whole chapter, which could be material for another book. I believe that I handled each troubling issue efficiently and by using knowledge gleaned over many years.

***

I have no regrets with any part of any trip except for one time. The last trip to Northern Italy included a two night stay at the Hotel Rocco Cavalieri, an amazing property. The plan was to stay overnight and depart the next morning for the city of Asti for the annual Palio, a celebration that began in 1275, and then return to the hotel for a wonderful dinner.

The morning began in Asti with a mass in the S. Secunda Cathedral and a blessing of the horses who would participate in the events of the day. The dark cool interior and a delicious lunch at the Brasserie Pompa Magna were a welcomed relief after a walk in the hot sun. This was followed at 2 p.m. by one thousand two hundred people dressed in medieval costume who parade through the crowded narrow streets. In mid-afternoon the palio (race) began. I had purchased tickets in advance for a group of seats so we would not have to stand and could all sit together and leave together.

Twenty-one contenders ride bareback around a circular track and are eliminated in three heats during the afternoon and into the evening. The rules include the fact that riders are bareback and can push other riders off of their mounts. A riderless horse can win the race. We found our seats under the blazing sun. There were thousands of people in the grandstand that held 5000 onlookers. A large area was dedicated to standing spectators.

The first horse, who looked more like a nag with his swayed back and enlarged belly, came trotting by us. The rider's legs were almost dragging onto the ground. People jumped up and cheered and that's when I began to giggle. As more riders came by, some going right and some going left around the track, my giggle turned into a hysterical laugh. There was no way to get the seven horses to face the same direction in a non-existent start line. When the bell rang for the seven horses to start, five horses would start, one would go the opposite direction, and one wouldn't move. Maybe it was the heat of the sun, or maybe I was just plain tired but I thought the whole thing was ridiculous and hilarious.

I guess I was the ugly American. After two hours in the sun, and the horses going nowhere, I signaled for all of my group to get up and leave. Everyone around us had a look of disbelief on their faces. It was a slap in the face of the fans sitting around us because they were so serious about the event and the American tour leader left laughing. I am sorry about that.

***

I found an advertisement in one of Terry's papers for a trip to the Algarve, Portugal, a place I knew nothing about. The price was right since it included air, a car, and ten days in an Aparthotel (studio). Off Jim and I went with map and tour book in hand. That trip endeared us to each other, to the land called Portugal, its flora, its unbelievably fresh food, its wine, its customs, and its people. While our friends spent part of their winter in Florida, Jim and I would spend our winters in Portugal.

In the beginning, not knowing any better, we picked up our rented black Fiat in the capital Lisbon, a beautiful city with not so beautiful traffic. We soon found out that on the main streets, the name of the street changes at every new block, making following a small map almost impossible. We got hopelessly lost. We asked a young woman, who without hesitation and with a big smile, threw her children into her car, after insisting on showing us the way to the bridge that carries travelers to the south and the Algarve. The Portuguese people are warm and friendly. After our first adventure we didn't fly to Lisbon but instead flew to an airport in the Moorish city of Faro, just twenty minutes from what turned out to be our usual beach destination.

Jim and I never mastered the Portuguese language but did learn the basics. Almost all of the young people can speak English but the older men and woman don't understand and just flash you a toothless and welcoming smile.

Each time we returned we became more familiar with the terrain, where the good local restaurants in the area were located, and where the places of history and tradition could fill many sunny days. We liked to stay in Vale do Lobo, an upscale community on the Mediterranean, where white stucco villas are grouped in the valleys along the azure blue sea. Rentals are more affordable in the off season because most owners come during the summer months. In the winter and spring many villas remain shuttered, so neighbours are few and far between. If you want to find friends, you have to import them.

We began to go to Sunday Mass in the 18th century chapel called Sao Laurenco. What's most interesting about this chapel, built in 1730, is its blue-and-white azulejo panels and its intricate gilt work. The local Portuguese parishioners cram into the few wooden seats, while the Canadian, Irish, and German visitors stand in the back and in the aisles. We seldom met an American. One Sunday Vitor, who was the priest's volunteer Sunday helper and very fluent in English, asked Jim to read the gospel in English. I did a reading after the Portuguese version was read.

This became a Sunday ritual, and handsome Vitor became our very dear friend. After Mass, the tourists all jump into their cars and head for the sea. The locals stroll down the hill to either go to the café to have a bica (expresso) or galoa (half coffee, half milk), or to the cemetery where a wizened old lady dressed in her winter woolen black, sells fresh flowers to the locals to decorate the graves. Many are buried in little houses built of mortar and glass, with a starched white- curtained entrance seen behind a locked iron grilled glass door. As you peer inside you can see immaculate lace bedspreads draped over multiple family caskets. Favorite children's toys are placed on top of the "beds" of the families young deceased.

I have traveled to many European and Eastern European countries and I always seek out a local cemetery. I wonder if somewhere there is a book relating to the burial customs of each foreign country. I'm sure that there is.

# PORTUGAL

If you look at a map of Europe, you can see how small Portugal is. The narrow strip on the bottom of the country is called the Algarve, and that is where the tourists flock because of the white sand beaches along the Mediterranean Ocean. North of the beach area are a series of low diagonal mountain ranges, each with verdant valleys of interesting small villages, orange groves and oak trees that produces the world's cork supply. Once a week you can find a peddler in a large white van who parks somewhere along the road in one of these mountain crevasses. The women, who dress in black and wear a traditional black felt fedora over a white scarf, all carry a large woven wooden basket. They come to get food goods or other supplies and to visit with their neighbours.

Don't be fooled about acquiring groceries from a peddler in the mountains. When you are in the Algarve proper there are several options to shop, depending on your mood and how much time you have. First and foremost are the two Saturday open-air markets which are located in small cities on either side of the beach communities. One market features two very large buildings, one that displays, on ice, all manner of strange fresh fish which have just been caught the night before. The other building has fresh fruits, vegetables, meats and cheeses. In between the two buildings are outdoor cafes where husbands drink some manner of coffee while hanging out waiting for their wives to make the best and freshest selections.

The second Saturday market is very Arabic in its design, including a traditionally maroon and gold curved Moorish entrance. It has both indoor and outdoor displays, especially of dates, nuts, barrels of olives, bright red strawberries and the largest, sweetest and juiciest oranges imaginable. Early in the season people can be seen haggling over the price of vegetable seedlings, caged poults and very young lambs.

There are many modern superstores available. Aldi's is popular, especially for buying discount bottles ($3.00) of excellent red wines. The whites aren't great. In a nearby village there is a German luxury grocery store complete with a doorman very close to a 'mom and pop' Portuguese store where we bought our fresh bread and cheeses.

Gypsy camps are scattered in many areas, usually at the edge of towns, where there is access to a road and grazing for the horses who pull the large wagons laden with all of their earthly possessions. Sanitation/toilets are not a part of their vocabulary. Bands of gypsies move their shabby camps with a change of weather, season or impulse.

***

On many days we would pack a picnic, take out a finely detailed map of the Algarve and head out for a day long adventure. Jim was always the driver of our little Fiat. We knew there were plenty of adventures down back roads that few traveled. That's what travel is all about.

Portugal has so much to offer, especially abandoned castles. One day we took off, map in hand, to find the sign that we had passed many times in our wanderings. After an hour we found the battered wooden sign attached to a tree that said Castelo. There were no houses and no people. We started down a dirt road that was rising upwards and getting more and more narrow. We now realized that there was a deep gorge located on one side of our car and the side of the mountain on the other. It was a Portuguese donkey cart wide with just enough road for us to keep going. We were both very silent. Finally, ahead, there was a small leafy arch which led to about ten houses on the top of the mountain, but no castle. The few stucco houses were closely lined together on either side of the one central dirt road. It was lunch time in March, and seven gray haired men and woman, dressed in dark heavy winter woolens, were sitting on a long bench which was placed along the stucco wall of one of their houses. Jim and I had shorts on. Their leathery faces were all tilted to catch the rays of the spring sunshine. They stared expressionless as we pulled our car up beside them. I jumped out of the car map in hand, and shrugged my shoulders saying "castelo?" They were all silent. We decided that maybe the castle was at the other end of the few houses, so I jumped back into the car and we continued on. After the last house we realized that we were at the end of the dirt road and the surface had turned to gravel. We started going down the other side of the mountain. The descent was even more steep and narrow than the other side.

A short way down I felt like I needed to get out of the car since my stomach was churning and I am afraid of heights. I stood with my back against the reddish dirt mountain wall as Jim turned the car around, patiently maneuvering the car, back and forth, inch by inch. After he got the Fiat turned, I got back into the car and we headed back up the gravel to find the dirt road and the village's back entrance. We stopped our car again in front of the seven bench warmers who were all howling with glee. I would say that we made their day, and as for us, we had another adventure and another story to tell. Certainly not our last.

***

Our stay in Portugal usually included Easter. One year we followed the Mediterranean sixty miles east to the Spanish border town of Ayamonte which separates Portugal from Spain. We had rented a room in a local hotel for Good Friday, and about dusk, we joined hundreds of others outside the Augustias Parish Church. We weren't quite sure what to do but two very nice people squeezed us onto a top step across from the church doors. In spite of how many people were waiting, there was complete silence.

The sun was going down when the wide gilt church doors swung open and about fifty genderless persons, processed into the sunshine. Each person was dressed in a hooded purple velvet robe, similar to the American Klan, the white supremacist hate group. They participated and walked in what is known as the Nazarene penitential procession, asking God for the forgiveness for their sins. Some carry lighted long white candles.

Next came young men dressed in black who were beating drums in a deep plaintive monotone. From time to time trumpets joined in to create more emotion. Their slow mournful beat would set the tone for the next three hours as it began to get dark. The slow-moving procession serpentined up and down the streets of the town.

The first float or "trona" came out of the church and into the sunshine. Spanish religious art is usually made of wood and always depicts the subject matter with upturned eyes and plenty of blood. The scene was a life size wooden sculpture of Jesus carrying his cross with Simon behind him. These floats can weigh up to five and a half tons. Many men flanked each side of the platform, sharing the weight which is distributed on long four by four square beams. The men bearing the load each wore an artificial Crown of Thorns, and many were bare footed. They feel that they must suffer pain to erase their sins. More floats depicting the Passion followed. The final float was a sculpture of a weeping Blessed Mother placed on a dias, high at the top of a set of broad stairs. Flowers were everywhere, and the stairs on the float were filled with hundreds of lighted two-foot candles which were truly impressive as it moved in the dark and narrow streets.

After the procession left the church, Jim and I drove back to the hotel, had a drink and enjoyed a traditional Spanish dinner. After eating, we went back to the crowds, following the up and down narrow streets. We could hear the sounds of the mournful beating drum up ahead. So much silence from so many people. We came to the town square which was located by the side door of the church. Three hours had past and people crunched into every available space. Many of the floats had already entered the church but the final float, that of Mary, the mother of Jesus, had come to a dead stop. Men and women were weeping. Then suddenly, a pair of windows located on the second floor of a building on the square swung open immediately in front of the stalled final "trona". A woman who is called a saeta in Good Friday tradition, came to the edge of the window and began to sing in a high-pitched operatic voice. Her song was plaintiff and very much in the flamenco style. Her voice carried to every corner of the plaza. She lamented for Mary's pain in seeing her son.

When she finished, the float was then carried back into the church where more people were waiting. I thought that Jim and I would be crushed while moving inside. Once in the church, the men carrying the float lowered it to the ground as the lit candles teetered back and forth. Each man was covered with sweat and ready to fall with exhaustion. The ambiance of the candles flickering in the dark, the silent devotion of the hundreds gathered, and the new cultural experience, made for an unforgettable impression.

***

Back in Portugal, preparations were underway for the traditional Easter celebrations in Sao Bras de Alportel, a small town located on the side of the second row of mountains. Our visitors always referred to the town as "Chicken City" because over the years we often drove there to enjoy a family style restaurant that specializes in Piri Piri Chicken. This Portuguese chicken dish is served with crisp salad greens and double dipped fries, and I swear that the chicken was always so fresh and tender that I doubt it ever walked.

One afternoon, next to the restaurant, I saw a flyer pasted onto a post in the traditional European style. The message invited people to come to town and join in the upcoming "Festa das Tochas Floridas" their traditional Easter celebration. It turned out to be another annual wonderful adventure.

In Sao Bras preparations begin at around 5 a.m. when people work frantically until Easter Sunday daybreak, so that when the sun rises it will shine down on the magnificent carpet of flowers lining the route of the procession. One hundred volunteers decorate the streets block after block, with 300 tons of flower petals carefully placed in wooden forms which have been placed on the ground to form a design. When the forms are lifted, patterns remain in brilliant colors of purple lavender, white and yellow daisies, bright green asparagus fern, and a myriad of other colors. Huge red banners are hung along the way which proclaim "Alleluia". Residents decorate their door with Palm fronds and white Lilies which grow wild in the area around the village. The pillars and altar of the Igreja Matriz (main church) are also decorated with Palm, white Lilies and red Roses. At 9:30 a.m. people begin to file to the church, everyone being very careful to walk close to the walls and other structures. No one dares to walk on any of the flowers carpeting the streets.

Mass was scheduled for 10 a.m. at the church located on the top of the mountain on a square at the end of a main street. It was standing room only, but in the square outside, men began to gather. Males of all ages, some very young who will keep these local traditions going into the next generation, carried a “torch” of their own design, made of a variety of fresh flowers and woven grasses. It was like old home week. The women were inside praying while the men kissed each other on each cheek, patted each other on the back and admired each other’s tochas (torch) handiwork.

Mass was over and the procession began. First came the men leading the way down the street with their torches held high. Then came the Boy Scouts and Girl Guides and then an um-pa-pa band. Then came a small float with a gold radiating monstrance bearing the host followed by a number of altar boys in long white robes. Next in line was the priest walking under a white and gold threaded canopy. I thought about the pale cloistered nuns who must have made it. The people who poured out of the church followed behind.

The procession proceeded to the central square of Sao Bras where everyone could browse through stalls selling handicrafts, regional sweets and nibbles, followed by a prize-giving ceremony for the man who had the best flower torch. There were also performances by local folk musical. By the time all of the flowers in the street had been trampled, many townsmen were thinking about the next year.

# SOLO

After working thirty-five years for the Niagara Council of the Arts, I had enough. I looked forward to a life of new personal paths. I knew that the non-profit organization had hired a woman to take my place and that the Board of Directors had fired her. Then they hired a young man from Buffalo. He, too, didn't fit the bill. In their wisdom they decided to legally dissolve the organization that I had worked so many hours to make a success.

Before all of this happened, a small group of people took on a very large cultural task. They decided to make the old and empty Niagara Falls High School into an Art Center. Some of this group were also new Board members of the Niagara Council of the Arts. When the Arts Council was having staff difficulties, I suppose that they thought that it didn't make sense to have two similar organizations. No one has ever explained to me what really happened.

***

I was always careful to catalogue and save newspaper clippings, pictures and slides of all of our past programs and events. When I left, all of the history, important files and past publicity was organized and in one place. When our organization was dissolved, all of those historic papers were taken to an empty nearby school and stored there. After a number of years that school was sold and all of the records, paperwork and PR was thrown into a dumpster and disposed of. It should have been transferred to the History section of the Library. All of the office and ArtWheels equipment was given to the new Art Center. The panels we used for exhibitions ended up there too. I have no idea what happened to the two vans. It's as if the Niagara Council of the Arts never existed. When I found out I was devastated. It was like disposing a part of me. I've always wondered why no one called me to let me know what was happening. One thing that I have learned many times over the years is that there are some things in life that you have no control over and can't change.

***

One thing I also knew I couldn't change was Jim's state of health. When Jim and I first lived together, his physician determined that he would need five by-passes. He was given a room in the oldest part of a very old Buffalo hospital. A wheelchair was waiting in the room to take him to surgery. This chair was as old as the hospital, with a high narrow wooden back, a caned seat, and over-large huge and heavy metal wheels. It weighed a ton.

I was there early. We sat on the bed and had a heart to heart conversation. He was nervous and shared his thoughts with me. He said that he wished that he had graduated from college and that someone had supplied him with the materials to attempt to be an artist. My answer was to assure him that all would be well, and I would help him do both. His feet were bare as he got up to shave. I moved the chair to give him a kiss, and ran over his foot, causing him to scream with pain. His message to me was to stay away from him till he was out of the hospital.

His surgery went well, and later that day a nurse said that I could visit him for a short time in Intensive Care. When I got there, the lights were dim, with only the monitors making that beeping sound. He was all hooked up. I bent down to kiss him and pulled out a number of wires and his breathing tube. Immediately sirens and bells sounded the alarm, and nurses and doctors came from everywhere. We both lived through the duel trauma.

After a number of months, he registered for college and started painting. He was so proud of himself when he graduated, and he had a natural talent for painting. It's sad that he didn't begin sooner.

We had been married about fifteen years when I noticed and could feel his left-hand shaking. We went to a local Neurologist. Jim explained that his grandfather, his uncle and his mother all had a similar shake. The doctor diagnosed it as Familiar Tremors. Ten years later we returned to the same doctor who gave us the same diagnosis. That year his general physician suggested that it could be Parkinson's Disease. We went to a specialist in Buffalo who confirmed that he did indeed have this terrible affliction. He began taking carbidopa. The shaking improved as we increased the medication, but other symptoms began to manifest themselves.

We looked back in time and realized that many incidents that happened in the past were all a part of this disease. He had a habit of choking on small bits of food. One time when we took a group to Seattle, I planned to have the final dinner in a very nice restaurant. While eating the main course, he started to choke, and I thought he was choking to death. There were three doctors with our group, and they calmed me down. After that incident we frequently had Jim's throat stretched. I was careful to pulverize his meals, and towards the end spoon fed him. As time when on, he began to lose more weight, finally loosing over one hundred pounds.

He would fall for no apparent reason, always falling face and arms straight forward. He also had a habit of blinking his eyes quickly when he was upset. I noticed that his driving habits were not as good as they should have been. He had to give up driving. A really sad day for him, but he finally accepted me doing all of the driving.

After a number of years his Parkinson's would not allow him to hold a paint brush or concentrate and this fact made him very depressed. He had no concentration for reading or solving crosswords which he loved. He had toileting issues. If he was really upset, which wasn't often, he suffered hallucinations and a few times became violent. My children had me hide all of the knives.

During the last eighteen months of his life I gave him care 24/7. I requested Hospice to come in for his final five days. I prayed for God to take him unto Himself and give him peace. He passed on November 8, 2018. I'm crying right now because I really miss him. He never complained, and he was so special. Everyone who knew him loved him. We had a Mass celebrating his life, followed by brunch.

He donated his body to the anatomical program at University of Buffalo. His ashes will be returned to me, then placed in a crypt at Gate of Heaven Cemetery in Lewiston, New York. I plan to be right next to him.

***

A new chapter of my life has begun. I am trying to live independently, although sometimes my body has difficulty getting in tune. I dare not stop moving. I putter and garden in the Lewiston Peace Garden where I can enjoy the outdoors, listen to the birds, and chat and answer questions about the flowers or our War of 1812 history. Gardening is universal, so we have many interested visitors from all around the globe.

Somewhat like Johnny Appleseed, I have left a trail of gardens since I have moved around the area. In 1987 I started a garden at the Red Coach Inn where we lived. Many times, tour buses stopped so people could view my colorful English garden. Some visitors asked me for seeds, so I kept a supply of small envelopes to be used just for that purpose. One of the highlights of the garden was a large hanging red and black wrought iron sign made by my daughter Mary Helen. It features a coach drawn by six horses and indicates the name of the building. It still hangs next to this English Tudor building just next to the Falls.

For a number of years, we lived in the penthouse of the Parkway Apartments in downtown Niagara Falls. In 2000 we invited a group of friends to join us on our porch overlooking the Falls, to celebrate the beginning of a new century. Amazing fireworks were supplied by the Niagara Falls Bridge Commission. I put in a

Gazebo garden at that building so that the senior residents could sit there and enjoy the ambiance. When setting up the garden, I could always feel many pairs of eyes watching out of the windows of that fourteen-story building as I crawled around on my hands and knees.

Now, I no longer crawl on my hands and knees but do my gardening contribution bending from a metal card table chair in historic Lewiston, New York. I am still a member of the Lewiston Garden Club and enjoy the friendship, knowledge and kindness of each member.

I'm now going SOLO (Some Other Latent Opportunity). What's in the future for me? I don't know. I know that I want to write another book about all of my travel adventures. So many of my fellow travelers put an interesting, sometimes laughable spin on our trips. I want to do an inventory of all of my art work and other household items because I'm not sure if my children know where some of these things came from. I'd like to do some more traveling. Then there is that 1000 piece puzzle waiting in the closet, which would be great on a blizzard winter day in Western New York. And I want to read…

Did Anna or Blanche think about their future, or were they too busy getting through each day, one with prayer and the other with moxie? All I know is that the SOLO me is not ready to quit yet. I have had a full, marvelous and interesting life.

I remember what Mark Twain said, "A man who lives fully, is prepared to die at any time".

# ACKNOWLEDGEMENT

I wish to express my gratitude to the Lewiston Writers' Group, to Mary Helen Miskuly, and to Mike Miller for their indispensable assistance, support and friendship in the writing of this book.

# ABOUT THE AUTHOR

M. Jacquie Lodico was born in Toronto, Ontario, Canada. She married and moved to Niagara Falls, New York, where she raised her six children. After they had grown she completed her higher education at Empire State University. She served as the Executive Director of the Niagara Council of the Arts for thirty five years. She operated Thibery Tours LLC for many years, taking small groups across North America and also to Europe.

She continues to garden in the Lewiston Peace Garden and is a member of the Lewiston Garden Club. She is a member of the Lewiston Writers' Group.

Made in the
USA
Lexington, KY

54439913R00120